Wonders of the World

The garden facade of Versailles, France.

Wonders of
the World

Edmund Swinglehurst

Hamlyn
London · New York · Sydney · Toronto

Acknowledgements

Photographs

Aerofilms, Boreham Wood 23 bottom; Heather Angel (Biofotos), Farnham 136, 137 bottom; Ardea, London 136–137; Ardea – Roberto Bunge 134–5, 135; Ardea – Clem Haagner 86–7; Ardea – E. Mickleburgh 145 top; Australian Information Service, London 150 inset; Peter Baker Photography, Crewkerne 29 top, 29 bottom, 35 top; Benrido Co., Kyoto 111 bottom; Bildarchiv Foto, Marburg 68–9; Jean Bottin, Paris 76 bottom, 79 centre; E. Boudot-Lamotte, Paris 27 top, 67 bottom; J. Allan Cash, London 17 top, 25 bottom, 34, 49 bottom, 55 bottom, 56 bottom left, 61 top, 75 bottom, 79 bottom, 80 left, 84 bottom, 88–9, 91 bottom, 92 left, 94, 95 top, 95 bottom, 97 top, 100, 102, 108 bottom, 114 top, 114 bottom, 115 bottom, 121 bottom, 124 top, 129 top inset, 142; Bruce Coleman, Uxbridge 38 top, 131 bottom left; Bruce Coleman – G. F. Allen 21; Bruce Coleman – Chris Bonnington 98 left, 99 top; Bruce Coleman – Gerald Cubitt 101 bottom, 106; Bruce Coleman – Gordon Langsbury 17 bottom; Bruce Coleman – Norman Myers 87 right, 112, 113; Bruce Coleman – M. Timothy O'Keefe 147 bottom; Bruce Coleman – W. E. Ruth 152 left, 152–3, 155; Bruce Coleman – Toni Schneiders 39, 51, 55 top, 60, 62, 63 bottom; Bruce Coleman – Norman Tomalin 45 bottom; W. F. Davidson, Penrith 44, 49 inset; Douglas Dickins, London 84 top, 85, 105 bottom right, 107 top, 109, 111 top, 119 top, 120, 121 top, 122, 138–9; Arpad Elfer, London 101 top; Feature-Pix, London – Gerry Brenes 73 top right; Feature-Pix – Norman Derrick 64 inset; Feature-Pix – A. Hustwitt 73 bottom right; Werner Forman Archive, London 103, 104–5, 105 top, 108 top, 112 inset; David Goulston, 25 top; Hamlyn Group Picture Library 45 top, 46 inset, 89 top right, 89 bottom, 90, 127 top inset; Robert Harding Associates, London 110; Bildarchiv Hans Huber, Garmisch-Partenkirchen 48–9; India Office Library, London 81 right; Luc Ionesco, Paris 107 bottom; David Johnson, Twickenham 124 bottom, 125; Mas, Barcelona 63 top; National Monuments Record, London 20 bottom left; Natural History Photographic Agency, Saltwood – Anthony Bannister 86 left; Natural History Photographic Agency – M. Tomkinson 82; Werner Neumeister, Munich 42 top left, 42 bottom; Photri, Alexandria, Virginia 133 top, 133 bottom; Popperfoto, London 128, 129 bottom right, 145 bottom; Josephine Powell, Rome 116, 117; Press Association, London/dpa: G. Rauchwetter 103 inset; G. R. Roberts, Todds Valley 147 top; H. Roger-Viollet, Paris 31 bottom right, 41 left, 59 top; Royal Astronomical Society, London – California Institute of Technology and Carnegie Institution of Washington 132; Scala, Florence 50 bottom, 52 bottom, 53, 58; Spectrum Colour Library, London 6–7, 14–15, 24, 26, 27 bottom, 28, 31 top right, 32, 33 top, 46–7, 54, 56–7, 77, 78, 79 top, 91 top, 92–3, 97 bottom, 98–9, 115 top, 123 top, 127 bottom inset, 128–9, 139, 140, 141, 150, 151; Tony Stone Associates, London 18, 33 bottom, 38 bottom, 130–1, 131 right, 146, 154–5; Swiss National Tourist Office, London 70 left; Charles Swithinbank, Cambridge 144–5; Tass, London 65 inset; ZEFA, London – Anatol 69 bottom right; ZEFA – B. Benjamin 52 top; ZEFA – W. Braun 96; ZEFA – P. Cotton 86 top left; ZEFA – R. Everts 20 top, 30–1, 61 bottom; ZEFA – D. Fröbisch 8–9; ZEFA – K. D. Fröhlich 40; ZEFA – I. Göbel 126–7; ZEFA – R. Halin 142 inset, 143, 149; ZEFA – Günther Heil 74; ZEFA – Heinrich 64–5; ZEFA – M. Idem 36–7, 37 top right; ZEFA – B. Julian 41 right; ZEFA – Dr H. Kramarz 119 bottom; ZEFA – H. J. Kreuger 23 top; ZEFA – Foto Leidmann 35, 83 top; ZEFA – O. Lutz 75 top, 76 top; ZEFA – E. Mariani 93 top; ZEFA – Puck-Kornetzki 59 bottom, 70–1, 72–3; ZEFA – G. Ricatto 148; ZEFA – Clive Sawyer 19; ZEFA – K. Scholz 47, 66–7, 80–1; ZEFA – Starfoto 50 top, 118, 154 left; ZEFA – E. Streichen endpapers, 42–3, 69 top right; ZEFA – Til 83 bottom; ZEFA – E. Vetter 22; ZEFA – Vontin 68–9 inset; ZEFA – Wolfsberger 12–13; ZEFA – G. Ziesler 16.

Published by
The Hamlyn Publishing Group Limited
London · New York · Sydney · Toronto
Astronaut House, Feltham, Middlesex, England
© Copyright The Hamlyn Publishing Group Limited 1978
Reprinted 1979

ISBN 0 600 39392 5
Phototypeset in England by Tradespools Limited, Frome, Somerset

Printed in Spain by printer industria gráfica, sa
Sant Vicenç dels Horts Barcelona 1978   D. L. B. 10369-1978

Contents

Ayers Rock, Australia.

The Pyramids, Egypt.

The Campanile and Doge's Palace,
Venice, Italy.

Introduction

Of the original seven wonders of the world only one, the Pyramids, remains. All the rest have disappeared; destroyed by wars, by acts of God or simply by disintegration through neglect. We cannot tell what they meant to the people of ancient times. Were they wonders because they represented some amazing technological tour-de-force, like the building of the Pyramids, or was there more to it than that? We are inclined to believe that when mankind chooses to call something a wonder it is because the object is symbolic of an idea which is of deep concern to us.

The Pyramids were remarkable for their size but they were also significant for the concepts they represented, portrayed in the tomb paintings and sculptures: the notion of life after death and, in a sense, the whole religious explanation of existence.

In the same way the Hanging Gardens of Babylon were more than an architectural and horticultural wonder because they stood for the idea of fertility and growth in an arid land; and it is by no means too far-fetched to imagine that the lighthouse in Alexandria was, besides being a large tower, also the symbol of learning – Alexandria was a famous centre of culture with the greatest library in the ancient world.

The seventy wonders chosen for this book, whether natural or man-made, represent the widest possible spectrum of human concepts and aspirations. Some of them inspire wonder because of their size or the technological skill required in their creation, but their real significance lies in the fact that they tell us something about mankind, about the inspiration of the individuals associated with them, and about the attitudes and beliefs of the cultures which regarded them as objects of wonder and still do today. For instance, the stones in the Vatican City tell two stories, one about the genius of those who assembled them into wonderful buildings, and another

about a great religious concept. Similarly, the Caves of Ajanta, the Shwe Dagon Temple, Angkor Wat and other temples and churches tell us about other religious philosophies.

Natural phenomena, though not actually the product of human endeavour, are also closely bound up with it. Mountains and water have been prominent among the places that are held sacred ever since man began to think about the meaning of his life on Earth. Today we do not ascribe religious meaning to mountains and waterfalls, but their significance in terms of the human spirit is not difficult to identify.

First of all they have become tangible symbols of the qualities of those who were their discoverers. Everest and Antarctica will always be identified with Hillary and Scott and the qualities of courage and determination without which they could not have undertaken these enterprises. Secondly, in the realm of the subconscious,

natural phenomena have always been symbols of humanity's deepest feelings about self and environment. In most religious traditions, mountains have been seen as the abodes of the gods, perhaps because they represent the idea of infinity, heaven and after-life, while rivers and waterfalls, the source of life for agriculture, have also been associated with gods and supernatural beings.

The ability to wonder at life on many levels is universal, and thus there is an almost unlimited choice of subjects for this book. We have chosen seventy from all parts of the world. Some are traditionally recognised as wonders, while others, such as the Centre Pompidou and Disney World, although relatively new, are pioneering trends in entertainment and culture which may become the norm while at the same time providing cultural continuity.

The universality of the objects and places that people wonder at is clearly demonstrated by the impact they make on

visitors from all over the world. Eastern temples, such as the Shwe Dagon in Rangoon, a living religious centre as well as a monument to the past, provide inspiration for East and West alike, as does the extreme refinement of the architecture commanded by Shah Abbas at Ispahan. Indeed here, perhaps more acutely than anywhere else, because of the contrasting environment, the observer becomes aware of the search for purity and perfection which is the basis of most art and an essential part of the human psyche.

Even such a static object as Ayers Rock can be, and is, imbued with a symbolic quality that most of the millions of people who visit it are aware of but incapable of expressing. Its very loneliness in the centre of the Australian desert gives it a significance that everyone can understand, whatever their ethnic background, and thus it is in a sense the very quintessence of the concept which has inspired our choice of the seventy wonders of the world.

The twin towers of the World Trade Centre (right) dominate the New York skyline, United States of America.

STONEHENGE

a mystery of the Stone Age

No one knows for certain why that huge circle of stones which stands on Salisbury Plain was built, or even where the stones came from. The association with the Druids has not been proved and may be merely an invention of the fertile imagination of John Aubrey, the seventeenth-century diarist.

The known facts are that Stonehenge was built in the Late Stone Age to early Bronze Age, that is to say between 1800 and 1400 BC, and that some of the so-called Blue Stones came from Pembrokeshire, while others were quarried somewhere near at hand. This is a less romantic explanation than the one put forward by Geoffrey de Monmouth in 1136 when he claimed that they had

been transported magically from Ireland by Merlin, the magician of King Arthur's court. The modern interpretation is based on excavations made by the Society of Antiquaries of London in 1919 and is generally accepted.

Stone circles were not uncommon in Neolithic times, and there are others in Britain and in France. Because of the references to astronomical facts in the disposition of the stones, it is reasonable to assume that they were an expression of a religious nature, since many early religions were based on the stars and planets.

In Stonehenge it is interesting to discover that the techniques used in the carving of the curved lintels suggest those found in Mycenaean Greece and Minoan

Crete. Could it be that those intrepid sailors of ancient times sailed as far as Britain and left traces of their culture? It would not be the first time that a dynamic trading nation had done so. Another similarity is in the weapons carved on four of the stones; these are hilted daggers in a style strongly reminiscent of those found in Mycenaean graves.

The design of Stonehenge is circular, and the whole structure is surrounded by a circular trench with fifty-six pits inside the bank. There are two further rings between the outer bank and inner stone circles, but whether these were of a defensive nature or merely decorative is not known.

are extremely large 4 metres (13 feet) high and 25 tons in weight, and that the surfaces have been worked on by hammers. There is also quite sophisticated work in the mortise and tenon joints of the lintels with the uprights and the tongue-and-groove work of the lintels themselves. This suggests an advanced craftsmanship which may have developed locally, or taking into account the Mycenaean references, may have come from abroad.

The truth about Stonehenge may never be known, but it remains one of the most mysterious stone circles in the world, as well as the largest.

Left
The size of the stones, the largest is 6 metres (24 feet) high, which awed the Stone Age worshippers is still impressive today.
Below
The blue stones which make up part of the inner circle were brought from Wales, crossing the Bristol Channel by raft. The largest of these, set at the centre, is the Altar Stone.
Bottom
On the 21 June each year, Companions of the Most Ancient Order of Druids keep a midnight vigil; Stonehenge, however, predates the Druids.

FACTS ABOUT STONEHENGE

Outer ditch:
  97 metres (320 feet) in diameter.
Inner circle:
  30·5 metres (100 feet) in diameter.
Sarsen stones:
  25·40 tonnes (25 tons) in weight.
  4 metres (13 feet) high.
Trilithons:
  50·80 tonnes (50 tons) in weight.
Tallest Trilithons:
  7·3 metres (24 feet) high.

The stones themselves consist of two circles, the outer one of Sarsen stones and the inner of blue stones. There are two horseshoes of mixed stones and an altar stone. Other isolated stones are the Slaughter stone, the Heel stone outside the stone circle and two station stones on the inner bank.

There appear to have been three main periods of building, the first was from 1800 BC and the second from 1700 BC. It was at this time that the blue stones were added. There was a final period during which there was a remodelling of the original circles with Sarsen stones brought in from Salisbury Plain.

The Sarsen structures are unique among the Megalithic structures of Europe in that they

THE TOWER OF LONDON
cradle of English history

When William the Conqueror invaded England in 1066 he found himself amid a hostile population that did not take kindly to his attempts to impose his Norman ways on them. To maintain order, he was obliged to set up strong points from which his soldiers could control the populace. The most important of these was a fort which William built by the side of the Thames and which became, over the centuries, the Tower of London, a fortified castle of formidable proportions which has been the scene of many important events in the history of Britain.

The Tower is not, in fact, a tower, but a series of fortified walls within which a moat, towers, and other buildings were constructed at various periods of history. Its entrance, when the Thames was London's highway, was through Traitor's Gate. Altogether, there are eighteen acres of land enclosed within the walls.

The central or White Tower, built by Gundulph, Bishop of Rochester in 1078, dominates the Tower. Built as a garrison and an armoury, it still contains the latter, including suits of armour worn by English kings. Within

the White Tower's 27·4-metre (90-foot) walls lies the superb chapel of St John, a Norman Chapel where many of the prisoners of the Tower said their last prayers or were laid in state.

The thirteenth and fourteenth centuries were a period of national turmoil, with powerful ruling families challenging each other's authority and striving to influence the king, and the building of defensive castles was widespread. Several towers were added to the Tower of London during this time, including the famous Bloody Tower where Anne Boleyn, Henry

On the landward side of the Tower a moat protected it in case of attack.
Left
The River Thames was the main highway to the Tower, and Traitor's Gate was the entrance through which those condemned to imprisonment had their last glimpse of freedom.

VIII's second wife, was imprisoned in 1536 before her execution. In this tower, over the centuries, were imprisoned Cranmer, Sir Walter Raleigh, and Archbishop Laud. Other towers of the Inner Wall, including the Wakefield Tower, the Beauchamp Tower, named after Thomas de Beauchamp, who was imprisoned there by Richard II, and the Bell Tower were all built primarily as prisons. The latter housed such famous prisoners as Archbishop Fisher, Sir Thomas More, the young Princess Elizabeth, and Charles II's illegitimate son, the Duke of Monmouth.

During the fifteenth century, the Tower played a part in the rivalry between the Houses of York and Lancaster. Henry VI, the half-witted old man whose reign had started with so much promise, was murdered there in 1471 and so too, in all probability, were the Princes Edward and Richard of York during the reign of Richard III. Richard's brother, the Duke of Clarence was another victim of royal intrigue; and he had the distinction of being drowned in a butt of Malmsey wine in the Bowyer Tower.

In Tudor times the Tower saw many stirring and violent events. Catherine Howard as well as Anne Boleyn were imprisoned and executed there, as was Sir Thomas More (who 'died the King's good servant but God's first'), Lady Jane Grey and Robert, Earl of Essex.

Even in modern times the Tower has held important prisoners, one of whom was Rudolph Hess after his unexpected arrival in Britain to offer peace terms in 1941.

For most of its life, the Tower of London has been more than a prison and fort. Within its walls many of the nation's important functions have been carried out. At various times it has housed the Royal Mint, an observatory, the royal zoo and the Public Records, and was a royal palace until Cromwell did away with the royal apartments.

Today it still houses the Crown Jewels and the national collection of weapons and armour. Six great black ravens still strut on Tower Green, for legend has it that if the ravens disappear, the Tower will fall.

DURHAM CATHEDRAL
Britain's greatest Norman Church

On a hill above a sharp U-turn of the River Wear in County Durham stands Durham Cathedral. This vast and beautifully proportioned building was begun in 1093 by Bishop St Carilef, who built the choir and transepts, while the nave was added by Bishop Flambard.

The distance from the Galilee Porch to the retro altar, known as the Nine Altars, is 120 metres (393 feet). In the porch itself is the tomb of the Venerable Bede, the famous monk from the Monastery at Jarrow, who recorded the early history of Britain before he died in AD 735.

The whole church was designed to be vaulted, and some of the vaults of the choir are prob-ably the oldest in Britain. Durham has been an episcopal see since AD 995, and its great Cathedral was erected at a time when the new authority of the Norman kings had not become firmly established. In becoming a monastery in 1083 Durham increased its power, and the bishop became equivalent to a feudal lord, governing the surrounding country and providing employment for the people. In Tudor times this power was curtailed, but revived to some extent after the Restoration. A relic of the great authority of Durham remains in the fact that the Bishop stands on the right of the Sovereign at his coronation.

WINDSOR CASTLE *historic home of the British Royal Family*

During World War I the British Royal Family adopted the name Windsor, dropping that of Saxe-Coburg-Gotha, with its German connotations, for patriotic reasons. The new name was eminently suitable, for Windsor has been a royal domain since Westminster Abbey conferred on Edward the Confessor the lands on which the castle stands. William the Conqueror, attracted to the hunting forests by the side of the Thames, built a wooden lodge there. Henry II began the famous Round Tower which is the most outstanding feature of the castle's

outline. It was Edward III who made it the centre for the Order of the Garter and also installed the Royal Apartments in the upper ward buildings. The work was carried out by William of Wykeham, founder of Winchester Cathedral.

Henry VIII added the southern gate, and later Charles II rebuilt the Royal Apartments and continued the north terrace which overlooks the river. One of the later buildings to be added was the Albert Memorial Chapel in the nineteenth century. Of all the castle's buildings, St George's

Chapel is perhaps the most beautiful. It is a fine example of the Perpendicular English Gothic style, and a fitting home for the Order of the Garter. The choir aisles were built in 1483 and the nave in 1496, with the stone vaulting added in 1528.

Many kings are buried here: Edward IV, Henry VI, Henry VIII, and his third wife Jane Seymour, Charles I and Edward VII and his wife Alexandra.

The castle is designed in two main courtyards or wards separated by the Round Tower. The eastern or upper ward contains

Left
Although provided with many splendid towers, the wall of Windsor Castle has had a more decorative than warlike past. These two round towers look across to the Thames.
Above
Windsor castle is still a royal residence. This is the exit from the living quarters.
Right
In this southern view, St George's Chapel is visible in the Lower Ward. The Keep in its central position dominates the 1·6-kilometre- (1-mile-) round Castle enclosure.

the Curfew, Garter and Salisbury Towers, and in the lower ward are St George's Chapel, the Albert Memorial Chapel and the Horse-shoe Cloisters. The splendours of Windsor lie as much in the great works of art by Rubens and Van Dyck and the priceless collection of drawings by old masters as in the architecture and its beautiful situation amid a great park by the River Thames.

ST PAUL'S CATHEDRAL
the phoenix that rose
from the Fire of London

The See of London was founded in AD 604, and St Paul's is its cathedral. Before the present Cathedral was built, various churches had stood on the site; the predecessor of Wren's great masterpiece had been one of the most splendid Gothic churches of Europe before being allowed to fall into decay and misuse in Elizabethan and Cromwellian times.

Christopher Wren had already made plans for the restoration of old St Paul's in 1666 before the Great Fire of London reduced the Gothic building to a heap of stones. Wren produced several designs for rebuilding before the so-called 'warrant' design was accepted. The agreement for this contained a clause which allowed Wren to modify his work as it progressed, which was just as well, as 'committee' faint-heartedness would have left Wren with a much less splendid Cathedral.

Work began in earnest on the new building in 1675. The main building was finished by 1698, and the whole by 1710. Whether the speed with which it was completed was due to the suspension of half of Wren's salary in 1697 in order to encourage him to get on with the job is a matter of conjecture.

The dome, which was to be the crowning glory of the Cathedral, gave Wren much food for thought. He wanted it to be Classical and massive, but to achieve this he had to solve the problem of the distribution of its weight. He did this by an ingenious arrangement of three domes, an inner one of masonry over which he built a wooden cone on which the outer dome of wood and lead rested.

Despite this triumph, Wren continued to have difficulties, many of them petty, with the completion of the work. First there was the aggravation of having the contract for fencing of the Cathedral given to a man named Jones of whom Wren dis-

Above
The choir roof with its nineteenth-century decoration soars over the choir stalls with their Grinling Gibbons carvings.
Below
In the splendid dome of Wren's Cathedral a succession of galleries appear one above the other. First the Whispering Gallery, followed by the Stone Gallery, and lastly the Golden Gallery from which energetic climbers can enter the Golden Bell.

approved and who was paid £1,000 for his work out of the funds for the Cathedral work. Then Wren was not consulted about the granting of a commission to James Thornhill to paint the dome. Angry over these slights to his position as the architect of the Cathedral, Wren ceased to attend meetings of the Commission which was charged with its care, and he was dismissed from his job as Surveyor of the Works in 1718.

Despite all the problems and difficulties, and the attempts by a new and younger generation to challenge his authority as the great architect of the splendid building, Wren was recognised as the true creator of Britain's finest Renaissance church. Wren himself, however, would have been the first to pay tribute to the great contribution made to the glory of his Cathedral by men like the Strong brothers, master stone-masons; Grinling Gibbons, wood-carver; Caius Gabriel Cibber, stone-carver; Jean Tijou, wrought-iron artist; Nicholas Hawksmoor, architect; and the many others who contributed to the creation of St Paul's.

Left
The clean classical lines of Wren's masterpiece are clearly visible in this side view.

MONT ST MICHEL
the Archangel's Abbey

The most spectacularly situated abbey in the world was conceived when the Archangel Michael appeared to Aubert, Bishop of Avranches, and commanded him to build an oratory on the island then known as Mount Tombe. Here on this conical hill, which rises in solitary splendour from the sands of the Brittany coast, the good Aubert began what was to become one of the wonders of the world.

The first abbey was built between 1017 and 1144 on the ruins of an earlier church, Nôtre Dame-Sous-Terre, which stood on the summit. During the next three centuries more buildings were added, including those places built between 1211 and 1228 to accommodate the thousands of pilgrims who flocked to the Abbey. These Gothic buildings, known as La Merveille – 'The Marvels' – include a superb group of almshouses, guest hall and refectory and cloister whose elegance and lightness makes them true wonders of the Gothic style.

Even the Hundred Years' War with England did not diminish the pilgrim traffic to Mont St Michel, and the English troops who held the surrounding lands gave safe passage to those who wished to visit the Abbey. In the fourteenth century a redoubt and defensive wall was built at the entrance facing the land, and

Left
The splendid isolation of Mont St Michel is best appreciated from the air. The abbey church was rebuilt in the fifteenth century after the chancel collapsed.
Above
The gallery arcades of the cloister are supported by fine columns that evoke the sky above.
Below
During barbaric times in Europe, the abbey cloisters were a haven for meditation.

after the collapse of the Church's chancel a new one was built in the Gothic style. The spire of the church was added in the nineteenth century, but it is all in keeping with the Medieval style of the whole group of buildings which crown the summit of Mont St Michel.

Around the Abbey lies the village, surrounded by its defensive wall and by the sea, which gives a watery protection except at low tide, when it recedes to leave vast expanses of water-saturated sands. Pilgrims through the ages have approached Mont St Michel over the causeway from the mainland, entering through the fortified gate and winding their way up to the Abbey by steps leading past shops and the houses where those who served the Abbey once lived. Here today shops and restaurants provide food and souvenirs for modern visitors.

Not least of the wonders of Mont St Michel are the superb views over sea and countryside from the 121·9-metre (400-foot) summit.

ÎLE DE LA CITÉ
the heart of old Paris

The island in the Seine on which Nôtre Dame now stands provided protection long ago for primitive man, who built his first settlement at Paris there. Centuries later, the Romans came to the island, and built roads, houses, amphitheatres and all the other symbols of Roman civilised life upon it.

The Cathedral of Nôtre Dame was begun by the Bishop Maurice Sully in 1163 on the site of an earlier church. The first stone was laid by Pope Alexander II, but the towers were not built until the thirteenth century. From then until the French Revolution the Cathedral thrived as the centre of religious life in Paris; the scholar Peter Abelard worked there until he broke away and founded the University of Paris. During the Revolution of 1789, mobs tried to destroy this symbol of the Church's power, smashing the statues and renaming the building the 'Temple of Reason'. In the nineteenth century a romantic picture of the Cathedral's life during medieval times was given by Victor Hugo in his book *The Hunchback of Nôtre Dame*.

The early kings of France lived on the Île de la Cité, and Philip the Fair remodelled the palace, now the Palais de Justice, a massive building with pointed turrets. Nearby is the Conciergerie, a prison which housed the unfortunate Marie Antoinette. She was one of the 2,600 persons who were sentenced to death by the Revolutionary Tribunal which sat every day in the great Civil Chamber of the Palace.

Happier memories surround the Sainte Chapelle, a beautiful Gothic church which has stood in the Palace grounds since 1248. This elegant building has over 1,000 scenes from the Bible depicted in its stained glass and several relics of Christ's Passion, including the Crown of Thorns, which is kept in a specially designed jewel box.

Joining the islands to the mainland is Paris' oldest bridge, the Pont Neuf.

FACTS ABOUT
THE ÎLE DE LA CITÉ

Pont Neuf:
    built between 1578–1694.
Palais de Justice:
    ceded by King Charles VII to Parliament, 1431.
    main towers – Tour de l'Horloge,
                Tour de Grand César,
                Tour de Montgomery,
                Tour d'Argent.
Sainte Chapelle:
    built 1245–48 by St Louis.
Conciergerie:
    famous prisoners include Marie Antoinette, Robespierre, Jerome Napoleon.
Nôtre Dame:
    spire 88·99 metres (292 feet) above ground level.
    37 chapels.

Left
The Cathedral of Nôtre Dame stands at one end of the Île de la Cité on the foundations of a Roman temple. At the other end of the Island is Le Vert Galant, a tiny garden popular with lovers.
Above
The Conciergerie, the prison from which Marie Antoinette made her journey to the Guillotine.
Right
The Great Cathedral towers rise 70 metres (230 feet) and house the bells called Jacqueline (in the small tower) and the Great Bell.

THE CHÂTEAU DE CHENONCEAUX
a fairy-tale castle designed by women

The refinement and grace of Chenonceaux stands out among a type of building generally associated with male characteristics. Though built in 1513 by Thomas Bohier, the mind behind the design was that of Bohier's wife, who superintended the building while her husband was away at the wars. When Bohier died he was found to be in debt to the state, and his castle was taken over by Francis I. As a royal property it was presented to Diane de Poitiers by her lover Henry II, who was much enamoured of her beauty although she was nearly twenty years older than he.

When Henry died in 1559 from a wound sustained in a royal tournament, Diane de Poitiers was obliged to leave Chenonceaux by Henry's wife, Catherine de' Medici, who gave her husband's former mistress the Château of Chaumont in exchange.

Catherine de' Medici, with her Italian love of the arts, transformed the Château, adding a gallery on the bridge across the River Cher and several other buildings. At this time the Château became the centre of a brilliant social life, and its masques and balls were attended by famous persons and royalty, such as Mary Stuart, Francis II, and Charles IX.

After this brilliant period Chenonceaux began to decay, and except for a brief spell in the eighteenth century when the owner's wife, Madame Dupin, gathered around her renowned literary figures of the period, in-

cluding Jean Jacques Rousseau, who was a tutor to her sons, its future seemed bleak. In 1864, however, a Madame Pelouse, née Wilson, dedicated herself to restoring the Château to its former glory.

Chenonceaux consists of a rectangular keep with elegant towers and chimneys, and stands on the foundations of a former fortified mill. A bridge with a two-storey gallery extends the building across the Cher River. On each side of the moat surrounding the main building are gardens, one of them known as the Diane de Poitiers' garden, and the other as Catherine de' Medici's.

In the building, with its rich collections of paintings and statues, many of them brought from Italy by Catherine de' Medici, are the bedrooms of its previous famous owners and a grand gallery, 60 metres (197 feet) long, overlooking the river.

Above left
The two-storied gallery was built by Philibert Delorme for Catherine de Medici. The great gallery is 61 metres (197 feet) long and overlooks the River Cher.
Top
The gardens each side of the keep were the settings for some of the festivals in Catherine de Medici's time.
Above
The entrance to the chateau is over a drawbridge. On the terrace are the initials TBK for Thomas Bohier and his wife Katherine.

VERSAILLES
symbol of Royal splendour

A dinner invitation to the house of his Finance Minister at Vau-le-Vicomte caused Louis XIV to build Versailles. So enraged was the King by the ostentatious style of Minister Fouquet's mansion that he had him arrested and commanded the architect Louis le Vau to build him an even more sumptuous palace.

Thus, Versailles came into being; a gorgeous palace, the biggest in the Western world, and surrounded by some of the most magnificent gardens ever conceived. But Louis had more in mind than an intention to score off his Minister; Versailles, some 25 kilometres (16 miles) south-

west of Paris, would also be a richly-furnished prison where the King could keep an eye on the nobility of France and ensure that they gave him absolute obedience. Versailles had been a favourite hunting lodge of Louis XIII, and Louis XIV had begun his re-building there on a modest scale, concentrating on the estate lands, where the famous gardener Le Nôtre laid out the grounds with fountains and statues amid formal flowerbeds and walks. Le Vau began his grand-scale rebuilding of the house in 1668. The palace became the centre of court life and of business combined with pleasure, and as the numbers of

the courtiers grew, of planning combined with intrigue.

The present-day appearance of the palace was largely the work of Jules-Hardouin Mansart, who gave his name to the style of roof which he invented. It was Mansart who gave Versailles its famous Galerie des Glaces, its Chapel, its great garden façade and its Grand Trianon. Other extensions became necessary when Versailles became the seat of Government instead of just a royal home, and government officials joined the crowds of courtiers.

What Louis XIV had begun, his successors continued. In Louis XV's reign the Opera was built,

Left
The rear of the Palace overlooks terraces with ponds and fountains and the park designed by Le Nôtre.
Above
A formal garden, called the Orangerie, with palms and ponds leads from the Palace to la Piece d'eau des Suisses.
Right
The Galerie des Glaces (Gallery of Mirrors) was built by Mansart in 1678, and has 400 mirrors covering its 75-metre- (240-foot-) long walls. The ceilings are painted by Le Brun.

wings were added and the Petit Trianon was constructed. More alterations were made in Louis XVI's reign, and the Hameau was completed just four years before the Revolution. However, in 1792, the splendid edifice was abandoned.

Today, the glory that was Louis XIV's France remains, lovingly restored, to dazzle visitors. Before the Palace lies the great square of the Place d'Armes from which one passes through the wrought-iron gates leading to the Palace courtyard. Around the marble court are grouped the buildings of Louis XIII's hunting lodge and to the right and left the wings of the Sun King's Palace which looks out over Le Nôtre's magnificent grounds. Inside are the grand apartments, sumptuously decorated by Le Brun, and named after Greek gods and goddesses: Venus, Diane, Mars, Mercury and Apollo. Outside the terraces, gardens, palaces and farms are the preserve not of nobles and courtiers, but of visitors trying to capture with their cameras something of the genius of an era which is past, but whose festivities and pageantry, excitement and grandeur are still present in the atmosphere of Versailles.

FACTS ABOUT
VERSAILLES

Louis XIII's hunting box built 1624; Marie Antoinette's model farm, the Hameau, finished 1784.
Estimate of total cost of Versailles, between £70,000,000 and £100,000,000. Construction involved 36,000 workmen and 6,000 horses. Gardens contain 150,000 plants, and cover 100 hectares (247 acres).

THE EIFFEL TOWER
masterpiece of the Iron Age

The discovery of how to put together large iron structures unleashed a wave of construction of large iron-framed buildings throughout Europe in the nineteenth century. The idea of an iron tower over 304·8 metres (1,000 feet) high was first suggested by the ingenious Cornishman Richard Trevithick, who was also the first to demonstrate how a steam engine could be used to draw carriages over iron rails. Nothing came of the tower idea until the engineer Alexandre Gustave Eiffel appeared on the scene. Eiffel was the world's leading expert on iron constructions with many viaducts to his credit. When an Exhibition was planned in Paris for 1889 he was asked to build something which would be a major demonstration of iron construction. He chose to build a tower. Preparations for it were begun in 1886; stone foundations were laid by the Seine on the Champs de Mars, a large open area stretching from the Ecole Militaire to the river. Forty draughtsmen were set to work making detailed drawings of the components of the tower, and a factory at Clichy began to manufacture them.

As the time for the opening of the Exhibition in May 1889 approached, the work became more intense and, despite the bitter winter cold, the hundreds of men involved in the task of connecting or riveting the iron beams worked long hours to complete it.

First the four heavy iron legs were erected and held together by a criss-cross latticework of

Left
Under the vast arch of the Tower is a view of the gardens and the École Militaire.
Above
The Palais de Chaillot, from which this view was taken, houses the magnificent Ethnological Museum.
Below
The Eiffel Tower rises 320 metres (1,040) feet) above the Seine. The bridge across the river goes to the Palais de Chaillot on the right bank.

lighter rods. At the height of 57·9 metres (190 feet), a platform was built on which the next stage of the tower was to stand. From here the work continued upward to the next platform at 115·8 metres (380 feet) and a third at 272·7 metres (895 feet). Above this was the rounded summit of the tower and its mast. Lifts were set into the iron tracery, and in March 1889 Gustave Eiffel hoisted the French flag on the mast.

Thus the world's most famous iron tower, visited by millions of people since its construction, and a symbol of France, was built. When it was completed, it was the highest building in the world. During its building, and since, there have been those who dislike it, but they are in the minority. Most would agree that Paris without the Eiffel Tower would be as inconceivable as France without Paris.

FACTS ABOUT
THE EIFFEL TOWER

Height:
320 metres (1,040 feet).
Weight:
7112·35 tonnes (7,000 tons).
Rests on four masses of masonry.
Contains three levels with lifts and a balcony.
From the top, the visitor can see for a distance of 90 kilometres (55·9 miles).

THE CENTRE GEORGES POMPIDOU

art in a crystal palace

In the centre of old Paris within sight of Nôtre Dame and a stone's throw from the Marais quarter, stands a glass palace that has become the focal point of the city's culture. Formerly an area into which the great Paris market of Les Halles spilled over, Beaubourg is now a place of studios and boutiques and craftsmen's shops. Above it all rises the sheer glass and metal building where all the art forms of the twentieth century have been gathered together.

In its luminous interior the arts of painting, sculpture, music, literature and cinema all have

their place. The Centre claims that no art form has been forgotten. In addition there are special study centres including an Institute for Research and Coordination of Acoustics and Music, a Centre of Industrial Creation and a Library with a million books, films, records and micro-index cards.

In the modern art museum are represented all the twentieth-century artistic movements which made a revolutionary break with tradition and changed the whole world's way of looking at life. Picasso and the Cubist breakthrough, Matisse, Braque, the

Surrealists, headed by Magritte and Dali, and the Pop art of Rauschenberg are some of the landmarks to be found in this unique collection.

The intention of the Centre Pompidou is to provide an environment in which the spectator can immerse himself either continuously or at intervals broken by meals, drinks or other entertainment. It is the unification of art which makes this a new and radical concept in the relationship of art and society today.

Above left
The amazing architecture of the Pompidou Centre sums up the extremes of functional and extraordinary modern art forms.
Above
The ultra modern art centre is in one of the oldest quarters of Paris on the right bank, near the Île de la Cité.

THE RHINE VALLEY
cradle of legend

FACTS ABOUT
  THE RHINE VALLEY

Wiesbaden to Koblenz:
  110 kilometres (68·35 miles)
Main wine villages:
  Johannisberg, Rüdesheim, Boppard.
Main castles:
  Pfalz, Johannisberg, Rheinstein,
  Reichenstein, Stahleck, Burg Katz,
  Burg Maus, Marksburg, Lahneck,
  Stolzenfels.

Snow White and the Seven Dwarfs, Siegfried and the Nibelungen, and the Rhine Maidens are three of the best-known legends that are linked to the part of the Rhine that runs from Wiesbaden to Koblenz. Once a part of the powerful kingdom of Burgundy, this region is thickly studded with hilltop castles that jealously guarded the rights of traffic up the river, which was the main north to south route through Europe during the Middle Ages.

At Bingen, near Wiesbaden, the Rhine cuts into the mountains and its valley takes on the character of a gorge; steep sides and overhanging cliffs hem in the river, which flows swiftly with rapids and whirlpools that once induced terror in those who sailed on it. The dangers were not only natural, for wicked barons often held passers-by to ransom, or dealt roughly with them if cash or other valuables were not relinquished.

Soon after Bingen there is a spate of castles; Ehrenfels, Rheinstein, Reichenstein and Sooneck. Here also is the Mouse Tower once owned by the infamous Bishop Hatto, who 'cured' his people's complaints during a famine by locking them in a barn and setting fire to them. They were avenged, however, as his own hoard of grain attracted the rats and mice from miles around, and they ate first the grain and then him. At the foot of the hills and climbing up towards the forbidding castles are vineyards which produce the famous Rhine wines.

At Pfalz is yet another castle which was financed by the tolls charged to river travellers. Then comes the Lorelei, home of the Rhine Maidens who lured too-susceptible sailors to their deaths. On the cliffs above are the castles of Burg Katz and Burg Maus. The former was built by the Counts of Katzenelbogen in answer to a

threat of the Burg Maus downstream.

Near Koblenz, at Marksburg, lies one of the most important of all the Rhine castles, the only one on the Rhine not to have suffered any damage, and a perfect example of medieval building.

Left
Stolzenfels Castle was built by Wilhelm IV in 1836 and its style is influenced by English architecture. From the keep there is a fine view of Koblenz.
Below left
The guns of the Great Battery at Marksburg Castle are permanently trained on the Rhine. Perhaps this is why it is one of the few German castles never to have been destroyed. It now belongs to the Society for the Preservation of Castles on their Original Site.
Below
Katz castle above St Goarshausen was the rival to Maus castle further along the river.

COLOGNE CATHEDRAL

the soul of medieval Germany

Cologne Cathedral was founded in 1248 by Archbishop Konrad of Hochstaden, but it was not completed until 1880. Nevertheless, the original design was followed down to the smallest detail in order to complete the grand Gothic concept of the medieval plan.

The site of Cologne has been important since people first began to live along the shores of the Rhine. The Romans considered it of such strategic value that they founded a colony there. It was not until the ninth century, however, that a church was built where the cathedral now stands. This was the work of Archbishop Hildebold, a chaplain to the great Emperor Charlemagne. His church was a double-choir basilica, and was fortunate enough to find itself in possession of the

relics of the Three Wise Men. These had been presented to the church by Archbishop Rainald of Dassel, Chancellor to Barbarossa, who had brought them from Milan. The ownership of such important relics increased the status of the Cologne Church and it became a Royal Church.

The Rhine was then the main artery of communication between Mediterranean Europe, with its maritime contact with the trading routes to the East, and Cologne, then an important trading centre handling the cargoes of spices and silks from the Orient and the wool and linen from the north. The discovery of America diminished its commercial importance, and traffic on the trade routes north and south dwindled. This was a reason for the halting of work on the Cathedral whose Archbishop had crowned the Kings of Germany.

Although some work was carried out during the fourteenth, fifteenth and sixteenth centuries, this did not radically enlarge the building. Two storeys were added to the south tower, and the nave and transept rose about 15 metres (50 feet) towards the planned height of over 42·50 metres (140 feet).

Nothing further was done until the early nineteenth century, when the people of Cologne began to demand that the truncated building should be completed. Goethe, the famous romantic poet and writer, took up the cause, and his considerable influence finally got the project under way once

more. This time the building rose steadily to the proportions which its designers had planned. The two towers with their elaborate Gothic pilasters were surmounted with lattice spires 157 metres (515 feet) high and the vaulting over the nave reached 42·6 metres (140 feet). The church lengthened to 137 metres (448 feet) and buttresses, pinnacles and towers sprang up around its outer walls.

Although one of the largest cathedrals in the world, Cologne is famous not for its size but for the lightness and grace of the style in which it was designed. The fact that the medieval spirit was reproduced so exactly is in itself a remarkable accomplishment.

FACTS ABOUT
COLOGNE CATHEDRAL

Height:
   161 metres (528 feet).
Interior height:
   61 metres (200 feet).
Length:
   137 metres (448 feet).
Main shrine houses relics of the Magi.

Below
The modern Roman museum stands on the left in stark contrast to the Cathedral.

Above left
The pinnacles and turrets of the massive Cathedral are clearly visible in floodlights that bathe it at night.
Above
At the far end of the nave lies the shrine of the Magi, and in the north aisle of the nave there are some fine stained glass windows.

NEUSCHWANSTEIN CASTLE *fairy palace of an eccentric king*

Ludwig II of Bavaria was, if not mad, at least extraordinarily eccentric. As a youthful monarch who had mounted his throne at the age of eighteen, he was greatly loved by his subjects. He had a sensitivity for the arts which made him an ardent admirer and supporter of Richard Wagner, but was not of that stern stuff of which rulers must be made in times of trial. When the Russians defeated the combined Austro-Bavarian forces at Sadowa in 1866, Ludwig became even more introspective

Left
Ludwig's ornate bed was appropriate
for Wagnerian dreams — or nightmares.

Below left
The grand hall with its heavy chandeliers.

Below
Neuschwanstein's pinnacles — a
prototype for all fairy castles.

than usual. To escape from the grim realities of the Middle-European power game, he turned to music and to building castles.

Neuschwanstein, perched on a wooded hill near the Alpsee, is the most remarkable of them, with its towers and turrets providing the prototype of all romantic Ruritanian castles ever imagined. The castle was designed not by an architect but by a theatrical decorator, and its interior is as much a stage set as is the exterior. Heavily ornamented with stucco, the rooms are like something out of a fairy tale.

Homage to Wagner is paid in the Great Chamber, the decorative theme of which is the legend of Lohengrin, in which the hero is transported everywhere on a chariot drawn by swans; in the Singers' Hall, with its evocation of Wartburg Castle, said to be the scene of *Tannhäuser*; and in the artificial grotto with its winter garden.

Curiously, Richard Wagner never stayed at Neuschwanstein, though he did visit another of Ludwig's dream castles, nearby Hohenschwangau. This castle, just as elaborately decorated as Neuschwanstein, contains a music room with the piano on which the King and Wagner played.

Ludwig himself does not seem to have enjoyed Neuschwanstein, for he occupied it for only 102 days. He was staying there when he was deposed in 1886, and soon after, he was found drowned in the Starnberger See.

THE ROMAN FORUM
the centre of the ancient world

For over a thousand years, from AD 800, the centre of the once-proud city of Rome was allowed to deteriorate. Grass grew through the paving stones where once Caesar's chariots had driven, the marble of the buildings was burned to produce quicklime and the rubble piled up to a height of over 12 metres (40 feet) in the squares. In the eighteenth century a revival of interest in ancient Rome led to the beginning of the excavation of the ruined buildings and restoration of some of their former glory. The result of the work of archaeologists and scholars since has made it possible for visitors to modern Rome to learn a great deal about the way of life of the ancient city.

Foremost among the ruins of Rome is the Roman Forum. The Forum was built on land lying between the Capitoline and Palatine Hills and bounded by the Quirinale and Esquiline Hills. The first buildings were erected on it during the period of the Tarquin kings and followed the war between the Sabines and Latins to which the legend of the Rape of the Sabine women belongs. Temples, shops and council chambers were grouped in three distinct areas representing the religious, political and commercial aspects of the community.

Of the early buildings there remain the Lapis Niger, a black pavement said to indicate a religious spot, and the tomb of Romulus, the legendary co-founder of Rome. Near the Lapis Niger are the remains of the old Rostra, or platform, from which the rulers of the day addressed their people. As the Roman Empire grew the Forum increased in size; the Curia or Senate House (the existing one was built by Julius Caesar) became the centre of government, the basilica was used for judicial hearings and public meetings, temples were erected to Venus, the goddess of love, Mars, the god of war, to the Vestal Virgins who guarded the sacred fire and to the emperors who in terrestrial terms were even more powerful than the gods.

By the time of Augustus Caesar, the Roman Forum was a splendid

place full of marble buildings among which the whole populace of Rome gathered to shop, to watch their rulers and sometimes to be present at the dramatic events which accompanied one or another political crisis. It was here too, that the spoils of war were paraded before the people of Rome to persuade them of the might and right of their civilisation.

In the time of the emperors, other forums were built in their honour. Surrounding them were places of entertainment for the Roman masses, such as the Stadium, where chariot racing and athletic contests took place, overlooked by the palace of Augustus.

Just a short walk from the Roman Forum was the Colos-seum. Named, some say because of the gigantic statue of Nero which stood nearby, the Colosseum seated 50,000 people and catered to a taste for every form of violence from the execution of Christians to mock land and sea battles where death was the price paid by the losers. The Colosseum remained intact longer than most of the other buildings of the Forum for it was believed that it symbolised Rome and that when it fell, Rome would also fall. However, in the end it went the way of all the other palaces and temples of the greatest empire of the ancient world, and its marble was removed and many of its stones were carted away for other uses. Partially restored, it stands today as a symbol of the 'Eternal' city.

Far left
From their palaces on the Palatine Hill the Emperors looked across the Forum. Immediately below are three columns of the Temple of Castor and Pollux and beyond them runs the Via Sacra, scene of many a triumphal procession.
Above
The Coliseum was opened in AD 80 by the Emperor Vespasian. It held 50,000 spectators and had weatherproof awnings over the terraced seats.
Left
The Arch of Septimus Severus was built in AD 203 to celebrate the tenth anniversary of the Emperor's succession. Scenes of his triumphs include the victories over the Arabs and Parthians.

POMPEII
the buried city

From the watchtower a lookout would have had a fine view of the countryside. The street leads down to the forum which is beyond the arch.

Inset
The house of Cornelius Rufus like most of the Pompeian villas had an entrance or atrium with a basin to catch the rainwater which fell through the impluvium, a square opening in the roof. Beyond was the peristyle or courtyard onto which the main rooms opened.

In the popular Roman resort of Pompeii in the Bay of Naples, life stopped suddenly in AD 79. Black clouds of ash, laden with poisonous fumes, rained down from Vesuvius as the volcano erupted. Most of the inhabitants fled in terror, but some shut themselves up in their villas, hoping that the nightmare would pass; in the end they died of asphyxiation. Their remains, buried by cinders and ash, lay under the shattered houses for 1,600 years before they saw the light of day again. A record of this disaster was kept by the Roman writer Pliny the Younger, who escaped and watched from Cape Miseno across the Bay what must have seemed like the end of the world. His uncle, Pliny the Elder, died with the other citizens. Today, the visitor can see much of the town whose end has been described so graphically.

The excavation of Pompeii, which began in the eighteenth century, has revealed the life of a Roman town better than any written word could do. As the buildings were dug out of the crust of volcanic ash, archaeologists found shops with charred remains of bread, fish, meat, grain and other foods, public baths, sports arenas, amphitheatres and even brothels. Villa after villa demonstrated the splendid life style of many of the better-off inhabitants, who lived in houses which faced inwards to a Peristyle, or patio garden. These houses consisted of a dining room (Triclinium), a living room (Tablinium), and an Atrium, or covered court, with a roof designed to guide rainwater into a central pool, around which were the bedrooms.

FACTS ABOUT
POMPEII

There were 25,000 inhabitants, 2,000 of whom are thought to have died in the eruption.
Excavated Pompeii covers an area of 1,000 by 700 metres (1,093 by 765 yards).
The Forum, centre of life in Pompeii, measured 146 by 32·8 metres (480 by 108 feet).

Above
The Villa dei Misteri was beyond the city walls. It was a luxurious house with murals depicting the initiation rites to the god Dionysius.

The centre of town life in Pompeii was the Forum, the complete ground plan of which has been uncovered. In this rectangular square with its views of Mount Vesuvius were the temples and public buildings and statues of the emperors. No traffic was allowed, but the marks of chariot and cart wheels in the stones of the narrow streets of the rest of the town indicate that elsewhere there was a continual movement of vehicles.

Even the political life of the town has left its mark, for on the walls are slogans and exhortations, so many in fact that at least one citizen was driven to write, 'Oh wall, how is it that you don't fall down with the weight of all this rubbish?'

Near Pompeii lies another victim of the Vesuvius eruption. This is Herculaneum, which was destroyed not by ash and lava but by a river of boiling mud which flowed over the houses. Less destructive than red-hot ash, the mud preserved the houses, which have now been restored to provide yet another amazing glimpse of life in Italy nearly two thousand years ago.

VENICE
a city built on water

It could be said that Venice is the most unusual city in the world. Built on some one hundred islands, it is criss-crossed by canals along which the gondolas glide noiselessly under arched bridges and picturesque balconies.

First built after the fall of the Roman Empire as inhabitants of the mainland fled from the invading barbarians to the island of Torcello in the Venetian lagoon, Venice rapidly became an important trading port. All the riches of the East were disembarked on its quayside as Venice, ruled from his pink Gothic palace by the Doge and his Council, became the cosmopolitan queen of the Adriatic.

Behind the Doge's palace lies the Church of St Mark, built in the ninth century and soon to become the repository of treasures brought back by the Crusaders from the East. With its mosaic-covered walls and its treasures, such as the altar panel known as the Pala d'Oro, St Mark's is one of the richest churches in Christendom. But it has its rivals in Venice: the Church of the Frari, containing Titian's mausoleum, and that of San Giovanni e Paolo with its sumptuous Doges' tombs, are two of the many whose towers and cupolas rise above the tiled rooftops.

The trading guilds and the merchant princes built their palaces along the Grand Canal, which snakes its way from the Piazzale Roma to the lagoon. Here are the Ca d'Oro, the most beautiful of all the *palazzi*, the Fondaco dei Turchi where the Turkish merchants traded by the Rialto Bridge (the business centre of old Venice where Shylock was spat upon by his Christian rivals), and the Palazzo Contarini Fassan which is known as Desdemona's House.

The riches of this truly fabulous

Sunset is one of the more evocative
moments in the Venetian lagoon seen
here with the Customs point and the
Church of Santa Maria della Salute in
silhouette.
Inset
St Mark's Church unites eastern and
western philosophies as well as their
works of art. The horses in front of the
mosaics over the main door came from
Heliopolis.
Below
Santa Maria della Salute Church was
built to give thanks for deliverance
from a plague hence its name, St Mary
of Health.

city are endless, and not all of
them are in Venice itself. Across
the lagoon at Murano are the
famous glassworks, and at Burano
lacemakers and fishermen ply
their trade.

The centre of this colourful
world is St Mark's Square, with
its Gothic colonnades, its tall
Campanile, which was rebuilt
after it collapsed in 1902, its
Moorish clock tower and the
cafés where all the world mingles
and gazes at the amazing spectacle of the world's most colourful
city.

ASSISI *home of St Francis*

Assisi is a small medieval town in Umbria perched on the side of a mountain overlooking a vineyard-covered valley. Since the fourteenth century it has been a place of pilgrimage and the centre of the Franciscan order.

The young St Francis, Francesco, was the son of a well-off linen draper and one of Assisi's wild young men before he became aware of his true vocation. After several revelations, during one of which he received the stigmata, he gave up all his personal wealth and founded the Franciscan Order with its vows of chastity, obedience and poverty. A brilliant organiser as well as a poet, he not only persuaded Rome to approve of his movement, but also helped a young nun, St Clare, to found the Order of the Poor Clares.

The spirit of St Francis and St Clare is a tangible reality at Assisi and gives an extra dimension to the many fine churches with which the town is endowed. The Basilica of St Francis is the most important building in Assisi, dominating the town from its position on a spur of Mount

Top
The Basilica of San Francesco is attached to a monastery, and consists of two churches one above the other. It was designed in 1253 by Brother Elias, a follower of St Francis.
Above
The single-aisled upper church of San Francesco has frescoes by Cimabue as well as Giotto.
Right
The Gothic style Church of Santa Chiara dates back to 1257. It now contains the relics of St Clare and frescoes depicting her life.

Subasio. It consists of two churches built one above the other, and a crypt. The lower basilica contains some fine frescoes by the early medieval painters, Cimabue and Simone Martini, and in the upper one the life of St Francis is recounted in a series of masterpieces by Giotto. In the crypt a simple but impressive tomb holds the remains of the Saint, which were discovered in 1818.

In the valley below is the Church of St Maria degli Angeli, built in the sixteenth century. In its Baroque interior stands the tiny chapel which was the first church of St Francis. This is known as the Porziuncola, and it was in this diminutive hut with its frescoed walls that St Francis consecrated St Clare as the 'bride of Christ'. The work of the female counterparts to the Franciscans was carried on from San Damiano, a small and charming convent which overlooks the valley. It was in this little church that St Francis was converted and began restoring the Church to its proper course enabling it to survive the later depredation of unscrupulous Popes like the Borgias.

The most complete and perfectly decorated building in the world was almost destroyed when the *palazzo* which adjoined it in the city of Padua in northern Italy was demolished in the last century. Only the protests of art lovers, including those who wrote indignantly to *The Times* of London, saved this great fourteenth-century masterpiece for posterity.

The chapel, now known as the Arena because it and the house to which it belonged were built on the remains of a Roman amphitheatre, was built by Enrico Scrovegni. The fact that an advanced artist like Giotto was commissioned to carry out the work suggests that Scrovegni was a man of taste and intelligence. He was also rich, and some believe that the chapel was built to expiate the sin of usury, since the Scrovegnis were money lenders – Enrico's father was consigned to the inferno by Dante along with other usurers.

Whatever their sins, the Scro-

THE SCROVEGNI CHAPEL
Giotto's joyful masterpiece

vegnis made a contribution to the spiritual achievement of man which is unparalleled in its beauty and human compassion. Before Giotto, art was stylised and hieratic, but he gave his figures a warmth and reality that expressed the humanity of their characters. Enrico Scrovegni himself is included, kneeling above the main entrance and dedicating his chapel to the Virgin.

The theme of the series of paintings which cover the whole chapel with their bright, joyful colours is the New Testament. Despite the pathos of the Crucifixion and the doom of the Last Judgment, the total effect is an optimistic one expressing the hope-filled philosophy of the Christian story.

To the spectators in Padua on 25 March 1305 when the chapel was consecrated, Giotto's work must have seemed no less miraculous than it does to those who see it for the first time today more than 550 years later.

Above
The simple exterior of the Chapel provides a satisfying contrast to the colourful interior.
Right
Giotto took care to record the donation of the Chapel by Signor Scrovegni.

Right
The fresco of The Last Judgement depicts the medieval concern and belief in the existence of the powers of good and evil and the rewards and punishments they reaped in afterlife.

THE VATICAN CITY
centre of the Christian faith

Although the Vatican was given statehood in 1929 by Mussolini, the dictator of Italy, its kingdom has always transcended national frontiers. As the spiritual home of Catholic Christianity, the Vatican has millions of subjects scattered all over the world. To them, and to many non-Catholics, the Vatican is the centre of the Christian world.

The focal point of the Holy City is the magnificent Cathedral of St Peter. Although now one of the most sumptuous religious buildings on earth, St Peter's had humble beginnings. In AD 90 Pope Anacletus built a small oratory over the spot where St Peter's body was buried after his martyrdom. Later, the Emperor Constantine, who accepted Christianity as the Roman religion, built a larger basilica. It was in this basilica that Emperor Charlemagne, who helped Europe to make its first steps back to civilisation after the years of the Barbarian invasions when he created the Holy Roman Empire, was crowned.

The present building dates back to the fifteenth century, when Pope Julius II, the patron of so many famous artists, decided that Christendom needed a headquarters in keeping with its status and began to plan the new church. It took three hundred years to complete, and during that time there was continual discussion about the form it should take. Bramante, the famous Renaissance architect, saw it in the form of a Greek Cross, Giuliano da Sangallo modified this concept, and Michelangelo reintroduced the Greek Cross and designed the magnificent dome, basing it on that of Brunelleschi's Duomo on Florence Cathedral. In the eighteenth century Carlo Maderno lengthened the nave to give the Cathedral the form of a Latin Cross, and he built the facade we see today.

The interior of the Cathedral

Michelangelo's dome towers over Maderno's facade flanked by the Bernini colonnades. The obelisk was originally erected on the site of Nero's circus where St Peter was martyred.

was decorated by the great artists of the time, including Raphael and Bernini, who built the vast colonnaded oval which spreads out before St Peter's. This Piazza is enclosed in three parallel rows of columns – 284 of them with 88 pilasters and 96 statues of saints. In the centre stands the obelisk brought from Heliopolis by the Emperor Caligula.

The wonders of St Peter's are rivalled by those of the Sistine Chapel, the private chapel of the Popes, which was built by Sixtus IV in 1481. Its ceiling and western wall frescoes are the tour-de-force of Michelangelo. It took him four years to paint the ceiling and another six to cover the west wall with the impressive 'Last Judgement'.

The museums, once the palace of the Popes, add the final touch of glory to the wonders of the Vatican. Here, in a number of museums, are some of the greatest treasures of the world. Books, paintings, statuary, scientific instruments, furniture and maps donated or collected by explorers, missionaries, Kings and Emperors, provide a superb feast for the many thousands of people who come to the Vatican City from all over the world.

Left
The Vatican Gardens, a haven of peace in busy Rome, contain the famous Villa Pia built by Pius IV in the sixteenth century.
Right
A view over some of the 43·6 hectares (108 acres) of Vatican City.

FACTS ABOUT
THE VATICAN CITY

Area:
43·6 hectares (108 acres).
Population:
1,000.
St Peter's:
211·5 metres (694 feet) in length.
Height to the cross on dome, 132·5 metres (435 feet).
Facade, 113·5 by 45·3 metres (376 by 149 feet).
Interior area, 15,531 square metres (167,181 square feet).
Sistine Chapel, 40·5 by 13 metres (133 by 43 feet).

THE ACROPOLIS
the great Athenian achievement

The Athenian genius for leadership had virtually eliminated the threat of invasion by the Persians by the end of the fourth century BC, and the Delian League which Athens headed was in danger of breaking up. In an attempt to bind together the members of the League during peace-time, Athens tried to establish the usage of Athenian money for trading purposes and the settlement of all trading debts and tribute during a great Pan Athenea festival every four years.

To provide the right setting for such a great get-together of city states Pericles ordered the rebuilding of the Acropolis, which had been sacked by the Persians

Far left
The road to the Acropolis climbs over a Roman path and through the Propylaea onto the rock platform on which the temples were built.
Far left below
The temple of Athena housed the statue of the goddess.
Left
In Pericles' time the Parthenon was a treasury as well as a temple, and originally, the statues by Phidias and his pupils were coloured.

FACTS ABOUT
THE ACROPOLIS

Parthenon:
Stands on platform 30·9 by 69·5 metres (101 by 228 feet).
Columns:
17 on each flank; 1·9 metres (6 feet) and 10·4 metres (35 feet) high.
Erechtheum:
Main block, 11·5 by 22·8 metres (38 by 75 feet).

c. 480 BC, and later partially rebuilt. Most important among the building plans was a great temple, the Parthenon, to house a statue of the goddess Athena. The architects called to take on this task were Iatinus and Callicrates with Phidias in charge of the sculpture. The building was dedicated in 438 BC, but did not achieve its purpose, for Greek civilisation was already beginning its descent into decadence and decay and the Greek city states had little compulsion to remain united.

During the following centuries this noble temple had a number of roles, as Byzantine church, Catholic cathedral and even as a mosque. In 1687 the Acropolis was blown up and severely damaged, and only the efforts of such men as Lord Elgin, who took some of the ruined statues to the British Museum in London, helped to arouse interest in one of the major monuments of mankind.

The Parthenon is a temple building in the Doric style raised on two steps. It rises to a great sculptured frieze 12·19 metres (39·5 feet) above the ground. The frieze, which decorates the upper part of the temple, is 159·7 metres (524 feet) long. The rocky plateau of the Acropolis is reached by steps and a splendid temple gate, the Propylaea. The architect of this was Mnesicles, who began work on it in 432 BC. The entrance has five gates with porches for entry and exit and adjoining buildings on the wings.

Other important buildings on the Acropolis are the Temple of Athena Nike and the Erechtheum, begun in 421 BC, with its remarkable porches added to north and south of the temple. The south porch, instead of using columns to support the roof, has statues of women in greek garments, the folds of which echo the traditional fluting of Ionic columns.

Despite its ruins the Acropolis is regarded as a symbol of the freedom and love of beauty which characterised the Greek city states.

THE CAVES OF ALTAMIRA
the dawn of art

In 1875 a little girl called Maria de Santuola accompanied her father on a visit to a cave near Santillana del Mar in northern Spain and saw on its roof a painting of a bull. At first no one would believe that these paintings were the work of the prehistoric men who had lived in the caves, but with the discovery of other cave paintings at Les Eyzies in the Dordogne a different view began to prevail.

The Altamira paintings date back to a time between the Aurignacian and Magdalenian periods (30,000 to 10,000 BC) when man was still a hunter who used stone and bone weapons to kill his prey. The paintings are in a chamber measuring 18 metres (59 feet) by 9 metres (29·5 feet) and there are about 150 of them of various types, ranging from simple outlines of hands to vividly coloured paintings of animals in red, black and violet. The animals depicted are those which primitive man saw as he roamed the hills and valleys around him: deer, wild boar, bulls and wolves.

The most striking quality of the paintings is their realism. Unlike later primitive art, the cave men had an instinctive sense of proportion and did not distort the various parts of the body as later primitive peoples did.

Many reasons have been put forward to explain why the paintings were made at all. Some experts believe that they were a kind of magic designed to give the cavemen hunters power over their quarry, others believe that they were painted to help the men to overcome their fears. Perhaps the real reason is that man had begun to reach out for an understanding of his environment, and had thus begun the long adventure in which artists and scientists have been engaged ever since.

Left
The bull has been a god or symbol of gods in many religions and to the Stone Age dwellers of the Altamira caves he was a creature that was admired and feared.

Above
The hunt was always the main subject of wall paintings which may have been a kind of magic to give him power over his quarry.
Left
At times, primitive man traced out his handprint but whether this was a game or a gesture that established his dawning sense of identity we do not know.

THE ALHAMBRA

an Arabian Night's fantasy

Above
The Court of the Pool is enclosed by finely designed facades which give it an air of tranquillity.
Below and right
The Lion courtyard is the most splendid of all the Alhambra's open spaces. Its name is derived from the lion fountain situated at its centre.

When the Arabs swept into Europe in the eighth century they brought civilisation as well as war. Their scientists introduced mathematics, chemistry and astronomy, and their artists a style of life which the medieval barons had never dreamt of.

Among the beautiful places that the Arabs built was the Alhambra in Granada, southern Spain. Here, within sight of the Sierra Nevada mountains, there grew up a palace fortress of astonishing subtlety and grace.

After the Christians had taken Cordoba in their war to reconquer Spain, the Arabs made Granada their capital and set about building a city in Arab style. In less than a hundred years they had lost it to the armies of Ferdinand and Isabella, who captured it from the last Arab ruler, Boabdil, in 1492.

Despite its unique beauty, the Alhambra was neglected, and parts of it were destroyed by the Emperor Charles V to make way for an Italian-style building, which was never finished. A great deal remains, however, to dazzle the eyes of visitors. The Alhambra consists of a fortress with walls and towers in red stone which may have given the place its name, since 'Kalat al-hambra' means 'red fort' in Arabic. Within the walls is the Alcazaba or citadel and the Alcazar palace. This complex of courts and halls includes the famous Myrtle Courtyard and the Lion Courtyard with its fountain supported by stone lions. Blue and white tiles, delicate stucco work and slim columns give an effect of lightness and colour. Off the Lion Court lies the Hall of Abencerages, where Boabdil executed a group of Abencerages leaders whom he suspected of selling out to the Christians and plotting against him. Above all, the Alhambra is memorable for the roses, oranges, myrtles and the sweet-smelling plants that perfume the air, especially at night, and which, perhaps, inspired the composer Albéniz to compose his suite *Nights in Granada*.

The beauty of the Alhambra is the more poignant because it was the last flowering of a Moorish culture which was already in decline.

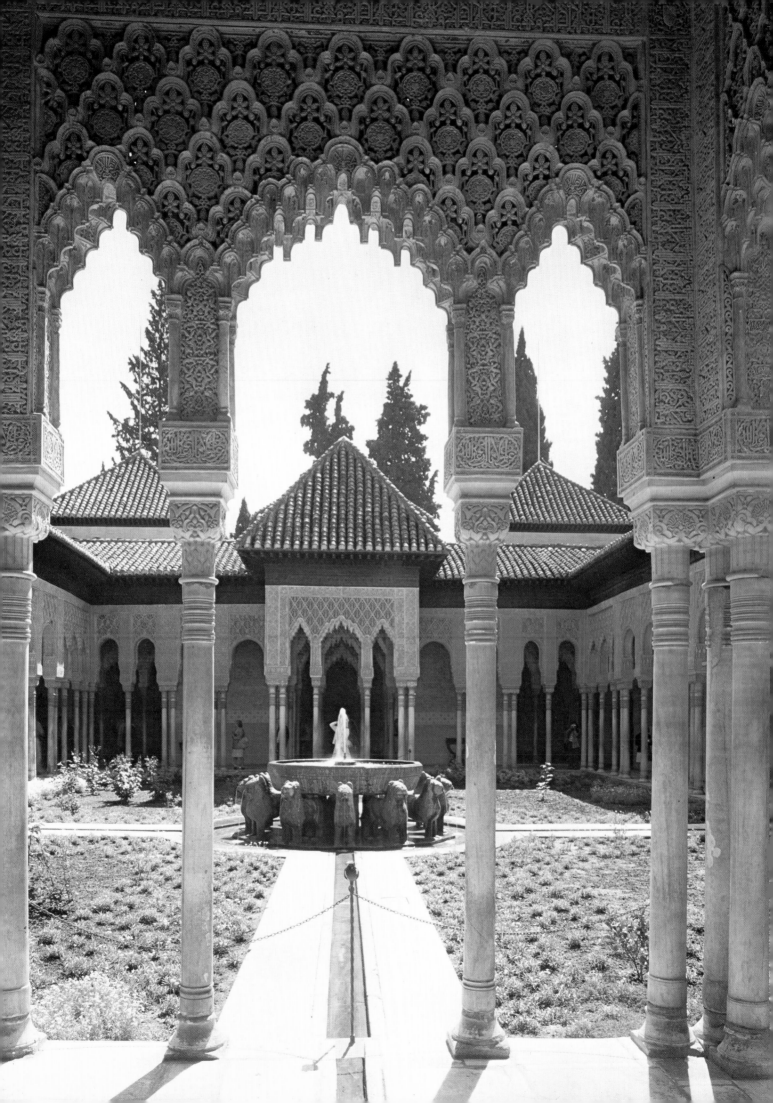

EL ESCORIAL

*austere masterpiece
of Philip II*

On St Lawrence's Day, 10 August 1557, the year after he succeeded to the throne vacated by the abdication of the Emperor Charles V, Philip II of Spain learnt that his troops had won a battle over the French at St Quentin. As a gesture of thanksgiving he decided to build a monastery and to dedicate it to St Lawrence. The building was also to be a Pantheon of the Spanish kings and to contain royal apartments. The site eventually chosen for this splendid concept was the Sierra Guadarrama, a range of mountains north of Madrid.

The architect appointed for the task was Juan Bautista de Toledo, who based his ground plan on a grid which would symbolise the martyrdom of St Lawrence. Philip II, an austere man with a burning ambition to restore the power of the Catholic religion, which led him first to a marriage with Queen Mary of England, and later to a bitter rivalry with Elizabethan England, decided that the new monastery and palace would be Classical in style. He thus rejected the elaborate Baroque favoured by his ancestors for their royal palaces in Austria and Spain.

On the death of Juan de Toledo, his assistant Juan de Herrera took over the completion of the great complex of buildings, and continued carrying out the King's instructions to create a building with the grandeur of a palace and the austerity of a monastery. The result is one of the finest buildings that Spain possesses.

In the centre of the northern side of the building rises the basilica, which is in the shape of a Greek Cross and is based on the plans of the Italian architect Bramante for the church of St Peter in Rome. On this side there is also a school. To the west lie the Royal apartments in the luxurious Palace of the Bourbons with their tapestries and frescoes contrasting with the elegant but sober rooms in which Philip II lived and died. To the east is the Royal Pantheon, work on which did not begin until after Philip's death, and the court of the Evangelists. The southern side of the Escorial consists of the monastery, and the library in which the King himself took an active interest, adding many of the 50,000 volumes which it contains.

Left
Aerial view of El Escorial with the hills of the Sierra Guadarrama beyond. The library and the monastery lie behind the sunlit facade; the Royal apartments and their treasures are to the left of the church.

Above
The splendid Philip II library has suffered from fire and the Napoleonic Wars but remains one of the finest in Spain with manuscripts dating from the fifth century.

Right
The east side of El Escorial once contained nuns' cells. The profusion of windows, there are 2,600, lighten the otherwise austere facade.

FACTS ABOUT EL ESCORIAL

Length:
   236 metres (258 yards).
Width:
   176 metres (192 yards).
Construction took 22 years (1562–84) and cost over 5,000,000 ducats. Building involved 1,500 workers. There are 16 courtyards, 86 flights of stairs, 88 fountains, 1,200 doors and 2,673 windows.

THE KREMLIN
Moscow's treasure city within a city

Moscow's Kremlin is a city within a city and its name, which means citadel, evokes the days when defence against invaders was as important a concept in the design of cities as their aesthetic aspect. As Moscow grew in importance in the fourteenth century, so too did the Kremlin. Much of its splendid architecture dates from the end of the fifteenth century, when Ivan III began rebuilding on a large-scale.

The Kremlin today lies inside a trapezoid of walls guarded by towers within which is an impressive number of palaces and churches. The tallest of the towers is the 73·15-metre (240-foot) Troyitskaya; it was through here that Napoleon entered Moscow in his foolhardy attempt to conquer Russia in 1812. Next is the Sobakina, 54·86 metres (180 feet) high and with walls 3·65 metres (12 feet) thick. Others include the Borovitsky and Spassky Gates.

Among the most imposing of the Kremlin's buildings is the Grand Kremlin Palace, rebuilt by the architects Chichagor, Gerasimov and Ton in 1838–9 after it was burnt in the fire of 1812 by means of which the Russians had driven out the French invaders. The halls of the palaces reflect the magnificence and luxury of the Czarist court. In St George's Hall, where the names of the great Russian heroes like Suvarov and Kutusov, the vanquisher of Napoleon, are inscribed on marble tablets, there are six chandeliers with 3,000 lamps, and the floor is inlaid with twenty different kinds of wood. Valdimir Hall, whose foundations date back to 1487, is an ancient chamber of the Granivitaya Palace which was built by the Italian architects Marco Ruffo and Pietro Antonio Solario. In the Teren, or Golden Czarina Palace, the daughter of the Czar received visitors. The apartments of the Imperial Family still remain, and contain silk tapestries, inlaid furniture and *objets d'art* once owned by them.

Among the most remarkable buildings in the Kremlin are the cathedrals: the Uspensky Cathedral of the Assumption, built in 1475 by Aristotle Fiorvante, where Czars were crowned and which now contains rare icons; the eleventh-century Virgin of Vladimir Cathedral; the Blagoveshchensky Cathedral of the Annunciation, with its nine cupolas, where the Czars were christened; and the Cathedral of the Archangel, with its five domes, where the Czars were buried and their likenesses placed above their tombs.

The great Bell Tower, to which the famous Boris Godunov added a gilt dome, is an octagonal 81·1-metre (263-foot) tower built in 1505–8, housing the bells which have tolled out for tragic and joyous occasions in Russian history. There are twenty-one bells in all, the largest of which weighs 70 tons. An even larger one does not hang in the tower at all, but rests on a pedestal outside in the square; it is the Czar Kolokol Bell, which weighs 200 tons and has never been sounded.

Today there are many new buildings in the Kremlin, built to provide council chambers and offices for the government of the Union of Soviet Socialist Republics, but the old palaces are maintained as show places for students of the history of one of the world's most powerful nations.

Outside the Kremlin walls lies another building which excites more wonder and amazement than any other church in the world. This is the Cathedral of St Basil, a remarkable church consisting of eleven separate chapels grouped round the central core. Each chapel is decorated in an exotic manner and topped with spires and the onion domes which remind the visitor that Russia is as much Oriental as Western in character.

St Basil's Cathedral is actually eleven religious buildings combined in one fantastic whole. According to legend, Ivan the Terrible blinded the architect so that he could not surpass his masterpiece.
Inset above
The onion domes of St Basil's rise behind a historic monument.
Inset right
Walls 19 metres (65 feet) high enclose Moscow's most historic building, the Kremlin, which despite sieges and sackings, has maintained much of its original appearance.

FACTS ABOUT
THE KREMLIN

Length of Kremlin wall, 2,194·5 metres
(7,200 feet).
Possesses 20 towers.
The Czar's Bell in the Bell Tower
weighs 203 tonnes (200 tons) and is
6 metres (20 feet) high.
The Czar's Cannon nearby weighs
40·6 tonnes (40 tons).

THE WINTER PALACE
a luxurious Czarist Palace in Leningrad

It was the notorious Empress Catherine who was responsible for the magnificent Winter Palace which stands on the banks of the River Neva in what was once known as St Petersburg. Breaking with the existing Russian style, she employed Italian and French architects to create one of the most superb palaces in Europe. Later she added another wing, the Hermitage Pavilion, which contains one of the world's finest art collections.

Catherine's Palace is Western and Classical in style, and is rectangular in shape. One facade faces the Neva and the other the Palace Square. Both the exterior and interior are highly decorated with columns and Rococo plaster-work which was put in after the Palace was damaged by fire in 1837. The restoration of some of the 1,500 rooms followed the original style, but others were re-decorated in nineteenth-century style.

Among the great rooms of the Palace are the Room of the Order of St George, where the First Douma (Parliament) took place, and the Peter the Great Room where the Emperor received the New Year greetings of the foreign diplomats at his court. The ball-room with its sixteen windows overlooks the river. In its glory the Palace was beautifully fur-

The facade of the most magnificent
of Czarist palaces in Russian Rococo
style with many classicist features
introduced by Catherine the Great. The
Palace was rebuilt four times and today
it is a museum.
Below
A view of the Winter Palace taken from
the gardens, overlooking the River
Neva. This facade is 30·5 metres (100
feet) high and 152·5 metres (500 feet)
in length.

nished, but much of it was damaged when it was stormed by
sailors and soldiers of the Revolution in October 1918.

Although again under artillery
fire in World War II, the Palace
has been restored, and the magnificence of its architecture and the
superb art treasures exhibited in
the Hermitage, continue to arouse
admiration and wonder.

ISTANBUL
meeting-place of East and West

Below
This old print gives an impression of the glamorous romanticism with which Istanbul was viewed by the Victorians.
Inset
View across the Galata Bridge to Istanbul, with the Blue Mosque.
Right
Hagia Sofia, founded by Constantine, is now a museum.
Below right
The fabulous Golden Horn lies on an inlet between the Sea of Marmara and the Bosphorus. The Emperor Constantine chose this site for his Byzantine capital.

The legendary Byzantium was the gateway through which the rich treasures of the East flowed into Europe. During late Roman times the city became the last bastion of a failing civilisation and the administrative centre of a new world religion, Christianity. It was the Emperor Constantine who turned Byzantium into the capital city of the Eastern Roman Empire in AD 330, and changed its name to Constantinople. He decreed that all Roman citizens should accept the Christian religion. The spiritual life which Christianity gave the city was reflected in the fine church architecture and the beautiful mosaics of its two hundred churches.

Chief among the churches built during Constantine's reign was Hagia Sophia, now a museum. This remarkable building was re-

modelled by Justinian and Theodosius, and when the Turks took Constantinople in 1453, the church became a mosque. It was as a mosque that it acquired the tall pinnacles which surround its central dome today.

Hagia Sophia ranks among the great church buildings of the world. Its most remarkable feature is the dome, a large flattened cupola made of brick which appears to float over the vast floor space of the church. The walls of the building are covered in many-coloured marble, and there are 107 marble columns supporting the vaulting.

Istanbul – the modern name of this ancient city – has been the crossroads of many cultures for thousands of years, and has many other wonders besides, including the Topkapi Palace and the vast covered Bazaar.

THE JUNGFRAU RAILWAY
tunnelling through a killer mountain

The north wall of the Eiger in Switzerland's Bernese Oberland has claimed forty victims among the intrepid mountain climbers who have attempted the ascent up the vertical north face. Until 1921, the wall was considered un-climbable, yet a few yards into the rock wall a railway existed which carried passengers in ease and safety to a height of 3,454 metres (11,321 feet) above sea level.

This marvel of railway engineering arose out of ideas first conceived in 1870. Various plans were put forward for making an ascent up the Jungfrau possible, including the idea of building an Eiffel Tower from which a cable railway would reach the summit.

A route via a tunnel through the rock of the Eiger was finally decided upon, and work began in 1898. After twenty-three arduous years during which explosions and cave-ins killed many of the workers, the railway finally arrived at Jungfraujoch.

The mastermind behind the building of the railway was that of Adolf Guyer Zeller, a determined romantic who wanted to provide the public with a means of enjoying the grand views then seen only by mountaineers. Guyer decided from the outset that the only way to get his train up the narrow tunnels was by electric power. To obtain this he had to build a power station capable of providing the current required. The engine of his train was to run on a ladder cog-rail system and pull a trailer car and lead car with 80 seats. On the route inside the Eiger wall, tunnels were dug and rails laid down. In two places corridors were excavated to the open air, so that passengers could experience the dizzy view from the face of the precipice. The first such stop was built at Eigerwand, a ledge used by climbers sheltering from sudden storms or other difficulties; the second was at Eismeer, the sea of ice, a sheer white sheet of dazzling snow and ice 3,159 metres (10,363 feet) above sea-level.

At the top station of the railway a scientific institute, to which Guyer contributed 100,000 francs, was set up. Here, work is carried out on astronomy, meteorology and physical and geological subjects. For the visitors to Jungfraujoch there are other diversions besides the mountain scenery. An ice cave has been dug out of the glacier, there are restaurants and a post office, and for the intrepid there are ski runs back to the starting point of the railway.

Left
The Jungfrau cog Railway (steepest gradient 1:4) starts from Kleine Scheidegg at 2,060 metres (6,760 feet) and tunnels into the mountain at the Eiger glacier station where a kennel of husky dogs is maintained to provide help for climbers and skiers on the snowy slopes.

FACTS ABOUT
THE JUNGFRAU RAILWAY

Length of Railway from Kleine Scheidegg to Jungfraujoch, 9·3 kilometres (5½ miles).
Gauge, 100 centimetres (39 inches).
Steepest gradient, 25%.

Climbing from Lauterbrunnen in the valley to Kleine Scheidegg on the Wengen Railway there are magnificent views of the Eiger, Monch and Jungfrau peaks.

MONACO
playground of millionaires

The skyscrapers of modern Monte Carlo dwarf Monaco and its princely palace that was begun in the thirteenth century.
Below right
The Edwardian facade of the Casino conjures up images of the Belle Epoque, the man who broke the bank, and those who did not and took the easy way out.

The few hundred acres that make up the Principality of Monaco have a long and turbulent history. Primitive man probably inhabited caves along the Riviera and relics of Cromagnon man have been found in the grottoes of the tropical garden. Way back in the year 1297, the Grimaldi family became the rulers of the rocky outcrop that juts into the sea on the French Riviera, and they are there still in the person of Prince Rainier III. In the intervening years, there have been assassinations and foreign occupations, and one of the rulers, Honoré, was thrown into the sea by his discontented subjects. During the French Revolution the Grimaldis were dispossessed but their land was restored to them in 1861 when Monaco was placed under the protection of France. In the same year, one of the successful operators of casinos at the fashionable German spas, M. François Blanc, opened a gambling place in Monaco and amid cries of indignation turned the Principality into a resort which attracted everyone of note from all over the world.

Today, Monaco consists of four quarters: Monaco Ville, the seat of government, La Condamine, the business quarter and port, where the yachts of the rich and powerful elbow each other for mooring space; Fontvieille, the quarter where light industry flourishes; and Monte Carlo, with the Casino, Opera, Aquarium and fashionable life. Every spare inch of land is packed with tall

The nineteenth-century 'Las Vegas' grew from a tiny, poor principality into a wealthy resort.

modern buildings, yet there are only 3,039 genuine Monegasques amongst the densely packed population. The rest of the 23,000 residents are all foreigners. Many thousands visit Monaco to enjoy the pleasures of Monte Carlo and the temptation of the Casino. The latter is forbidden to the true citizen of Monaco, whose compensation is that he pays no income tax nor death duties.

THE PYRAMIDS
tombs of the Pharaohs

The Pyramids, the biggest tombs ever built, were more than just places in which the bodies of Egypt's pharaohs were preserved for the afterlife. They were visible symbols of the whole power of ancient Egyptian civilisation.

This civilisation, which lasted over 4,000 years, was bound together by a rigid hierarchical structure which applied as much to the rulers as to the people. Its ethos was provided by a priestly caste who were not only the arbiters of spiritual life, but controlled much of the secular life as well. The priests were the men of letters, government advisers and scientists; a kind of early civil service whose role was to preserve the established society and to protect its continuity. In this, the pyramid played a part in death, as the palaces did in life. The palaces with their huge columns and statues were built to impress the people with the power of their rulers in life; the pyramids affirmed this power in death.

The building of pyramids be-

For many years the 20-metre- (66-foot-) high Sphinx was almost covered with sand. Here it is with Chefrens pyramid in the background.
Right
Cheops and Chefrens pyramids are of a similar height 146 metres (480 feet) and 143 metres (470 feet) respectively, but Mycerinos measures a mere 66·5 metres (218 feet).
Below right
The pyramid of Cheops was once covered by a smooth layer of granite.

gan in the time of the Old Kingdom (2613 BC) and developed from the *mastaba*, a flat-topped rectangular mud or brick superstructure built over a burial chamber. It was the pharaoh Djoser of the Third Dynasty who built the first stone *mastaba*, and he staggered the walls in steps which rose to 60 metres (196·8 feet). This was at Saggarah, and it was near here that a Fourth Dynasty pharaoh, Sneferu, also built a pyramid-shaped tomb. The same pharaoh developed the

pyramid concept at Mazdum by filling in the steps of the *mastaba*, thus creating a smooth pyramid shape. The size of the pyramids grew as the concept was developed until the great pyramids at Gizeh were built by the pharaohs Cheops, Chephren and Mycerinos.

These pharaohs, about whom little is known, cannot have seen the work completed in their lifetime. The building of the great pyramids was accomplished by thousands of workers dragging the huge stones, weighing as much

as 2½ tons, up earth ramps to the required height.

The great pyramid of Cheops had a height of 156·59 metres (514·6 feet), now worn down a few feet, and a base of 230 metres (754·5 feet) square. It is made up of 2,300,000 blocks of stone, and its entrance on the north side is 18 metres (59·04 feet) above ground. A corridor leads down to an underground chamber from which there is an ascent to the Queen's chamber and then the King's chamber.

FACTS ABOUT
THE PYRAMIDS

Cheops:
146·30 metres (480 feet) high
Queen's Chamber:
21 metres (70 feet) above ground.
King's Chamber:
5·2 by 105 metres (17·2 by 34·4 feet).
Chefren:
143 metres high (470 feet).
Mycerinos:
66·5 metres high (218 feet).
Sphinx:
73·2 metres (240 feet) long.
20 metres (66 feet) high.

THEBES
palaces and tombs of the Pharaohs

As the ancient Egyptians began to explore and conquer the territories of Nubia, Ethiopia and Libya which lay within reach of the Nile they decided to move their capital city from Memphis to a more convenient place up river. About 2160 BC, they chose Thebes, lying between the Libyan and Arabian deserts, as the place for their new city.

To honour their chief god Amon they built temples, and to display their power and impress their subject peoples they erected vast palaces. The greatest of these were built by their warrior kings, Tutmosis III, Amenofis III, Rameses II and Rameses III. Everything in the new city was planned on a colossal size. The Temple of Luxor, for instance, was 260 metres (853 feet) long and had six huge figures of

Rameses II standing before it. In Karnak, nearby, Queen Hatshephut erected tall obelisks outside the building made for her brother and husband Tutmosis III.

The pharaohs kept their power and divine authority closely guarded. They were aided by priests, who were administrators and scientists whose knowledge of natural phenomena they ascribed to divine communication. This union of state and religion was perpetuated even in death, and the necropolis at Thebes was as important as the palaces. Here the pharaohs were buried in vast mausoleums dug out of the hillsides together with buried household treasures, precious stones and even their servants and animals. The most famous of these is that of Tutankhamen,

discovered in 1922.

Such hidden wealth was a temptation to grave robbers, and many of the treasures have disappeared. The investigation of the tombs in the nineteenth and twentieth centuries increased the pillage of the ancient tombs, but enough has been left and preserved in museums to reveal to the world the wonders of one of the longest-lived civilisations on earth.

FACTS ABOUT
THEBES

Capital of ancient Egypt 2190–2040 BC.
Abu Simbel:
Facade of the Great Temple:
    36 metres (119 feet) wide.
    32 metres (105 feet) high.
Statues of Rameses:
    20 metres (65 feet) high.
Temple of Amon, Karnak:
    366 metres by 100 metres (1,200
    feet by 328 feet).

Above left
Rameses II, the great warrior King, built this Temple to the god Amon.
Far left
The sculptures at Thebes are some of the finest in Egyptian art.
Above
The most imposing of all the tombs in the Valley of Kings is that of Queen Hatsheput at Deir-el-Bahari.

THE ASWAN HIGH DAM
controlling the life blood of Egypt

The waters of the Nile made possible the foundation of the longest-lived and most successful of the world's civilisations. A knowledge of irrigation and understanding of the rise and fall of the Nile waters was an important element in the government of the ancient Egyptian nation.

It is only recently, however, that control of the Nile waters has become a reality through the construction of dams which provide reserves of water for irrigation and hydroelectric power.

The largest dam to be built on the Nile and one of the biggest reservoirs of water in the world is the Aswan High Dam. The wall of the dam, completed in 1970, holds back some 157 million cubic metres (205 million cubic yards) of water over 644 kilometres (400 miles) of river valley. As the water piled up behind the dam the 90,000 people who lived in the valley had to be re-settled in new lands in Egypt and the Sudan, while various organisations throughout the world set about finding ways to save the ancient buildings that would be covered by the floodwaters.

One of the most important of the fifteen temples that had to be rescued was Abu Simbel. At this place, the temple of Rameses II and Queen Nefertari had been hewn out of the rock and the problems involved in moving them were prodigious. UNESCO and twenty nations contributed to this great project. The work took several years to complete, and during this time the temples were cut away from the rock face and transported piece by piece to a site 61 metres (200 feet) higher up the cliff.

The new dam will bring back to Aswan its historical importance in a new way. No longer a garrison town as in the time of the Romans, when they kept troops stationed on Elephantine Island, nor simply a place where granite was quarried for the Egyptian temples, Aswan and its High Dam have now become the place where the life-giving waters of the Nile will be controlled and put to work for the benefit of the whole of Egypt.

Left
The colossal structures guarding the
Temple of Ramses at Abu Simbel were
saved from submersion in the rising
waters behind the Aswan Dam and
moved piece by piece to their present
location.
Above
The High Dam is upstream from the
existing Aswan Dam.

Left
Abu Simbel; the statues are being
moved to their new location.
Below
The construction of the Dam has
rationalised the life of the Egyptian
farmer who is no longer subject to the
varying river flow.

THE SUEZ CANAL

corridor to the East

For centuries the only communication between Europe and the East was by arduous caravan routes across the deserts of the Middle East and Asia. Then came the ships of European merchant adventurers. Once travel by sea had become more secure and regular, cargoes and people were transported by the famous Overland Route from Port Said to Suez where they were embarked on ships sailing to the East.

The idea of a canal to link the Mediterranean and the Red Sea, and thus open an even better route to the Indian Ocean, was not new. The Ptolemys of ancient Egypt had thought of it, and so had the Venetians in the fifteenth century. Nothing concrete was done until Napoleon ordered a canal survey to be made.

In 1854 Fernand de Lesseps obtained the approval of the Khedive of Egypt for his great project to build a canal, and a Suez Canal Company was formed with the financial participation of France.

Above
The expression 'posh' is derived from the situation of cabins in the ships that sailed from England to the East (port-side out, starboard home) at the height of Britain's imperial power.
Right
The Great Bitter Lake lies on the route from Port Said to Suez. When the Canal was opened in 1869 its 160 kilometres (90 miles) shortened the journey to the Middle East by thousands of kilometres.
Far right
The reopening of the Canal will not restore the traffic of the great days of sea transport but it will make cruising possible in the Red Sea.

The Canal was opened in 1869 in the presence of the Empress Eugenie. Tourists crowded to see the Canal, among them the Prince of Wales and the first party Thomas Cook took to Egypt. Giuseppe Verdi's opera, *Aida*, was commissioned to mark the event, but was not finished in time.

De Lesseps' Canal was 6 metres (19·6 feet) deep and 22 metres (72·1 feet) wide, and in its early years ships were constantly running aground: between 1870 and 1884 no fewer than 3,000 of them encountered such difficulties.

Great Britain acquired an interest in the Canal almost equal to that of France when the Khedive ran into money difficulties and sold his shares in the Suez Company in 1875. The raising of the necessary £4,500,000 to buy the shares was one of Benjamin Disraeli's great coups as Prime Minister. Britain and France both lost their hold on the Canal in the Suez Crisis of 1956.

In 1870 486 transits of the Canal were made; just before the Arab–Israeli War of 1967 closed the Canal, transits numbered 20,336 in the year. Although the Canal has been cleared of the debris of war and re-opened, increasing air transport and the huge size of the great oil tankers which makes them use the Cape route rather than Suez, means that the Canal will probably never know its former glories again.

FACTS ABOUT
THE SUEZ CANAL

Port Said to Suez:
  160 kilometres (99·4 miles).
Present width:
  152·4 metres (500 feet) at surface.
Present depth:
  12·19 metres (40 feet).
Normal transit time:
  13 hours.

MOUNT KILIMANJARO
a snow-covered volcano on the Equator

Situated between Tanzania and Kenya on latitude 3° 4'S, Kilimanjaro has fascinated explorers and writers ever since it was discovered by the German missionaries Johannes Rebman and Ludwig Krapf in 1848.

The mountain has two peaks, both of them dormant volcanoes. Kibo, the higher, is the highest peak in Africa. It has a huge crater within which there is a secondary cone, 113 metres (370 feet) across and 122 metres (400 feet) deep. On Kibo there are still signs of volcanic activity in the solfataras which exude sulphurous smoke. Mawensi, the other peak, appears to be extinct. Its volcanic cone has been withered away into ridges of jagged rocks climbable only by experienced mountaineers.

Kibo can be ascended more easily, and the journey upwards takes the climber through a variety of distinct areas of vegetation, corresponding to the climatic zones. At the foot are tropical farmlands where coffee and banana plantations flourish, temperate forests appear at the cloud level, and near the snow line there is bare scrubby land.

On the lower slopes of Kilimanjaro wild animals roam freely in a nature reserve; elephant, rhino, buffalo and antelope abound and add to the picture of a world which has changed little since man was a hunter.

Left
From the Amboseli game reserve,
Kilimanjaro stands out as a landmark.
Above
Kenyans and visitors alike enjoy the
long walk up to Mawensi through dry
grasslands where cacti grow, to the
temperate regions at a higher level.
Right
Kiwo is a rough, crumbling peak which
is difficult to ascend. The approach
through dry scrubland is not particularly
attractive either.

THE VICTORIA FALLS
the smoke that thunders

Above
The spectacular gorge into which the Falls pour is 64 metres (210 feet) wide and 118·8 metres (390 feet) long.
Right
The water flowing at an average rate of 934·42 cubic metres (33,000 cubic feet) per second hits the gorge walls with a thunderous roar.
Far right
A rainbow hovers over the Zambesi River on the Rhodesian side of the Falls.

When Dr Livingstone discovered the great falls that crash down a chasm in the Zambesi River in 1855 he was 'stunned with amazement'. His first intimations of the existence of the falls were the plumes of spray that rise above them and the thunder of water pouring into the gorge below.

The object of Dr Livingstone's surprise was caused by the extraordinary geological formation of the river bed, which suddenly disappears into a deep cleft from which the only escape is a narrow gorge in the opposite wall. The water arriving with great force becomes a seething cauldron from which a drenching spray rises and saturates the rain forest facing the Falls.

The Victoria Falls themselves, separated by small islands, are 1,370 metres (4,495 feet) across. At the western end is the Devil's Cataract, then comes Cataract Island, followed by the main falls. To the east of these are the Rainbow Falls and at the eastern end is the Eastern Cataract.

As the river finds its way down the narrow Batoka Gorge in a tumult of water, suitably named the Boiling Pot, it flows under the railway bridge linking Rhodesia and Zambia. The countryside around the Falls is much as in the days of Dr Livingstone, and wild game roam in the nearby national parks.

FACTS ABOUT
THE VICTORIA FALLS

Height:
107 metres (355 feet).
Width: 1,370 metres (4,495 feet).
Volume of water (maximum flow):
4 million cubic metres (140 million cubic feet), depending on season. Water hits opposite wall of chasm 24–73 metres (80–240 feet) up.

THE OKAVANGO SWAMP
the river that disappeared

The Okavango River rises in Angola, and after a journey of 1,600 kilometres (994.1 miles) it simply disappears into the Kalahari desert in a vast swampland the edges of which are cracked and sunbaked earth scorched by the sun.

On the Bie Plateau, where the river rises, it is called the Cubango, and flows through a steep wooded valley, sometimes rushing headlong over rapids and at others wending its way under tropical forests. At the Popa Falls on the edge of the plateau the river descends rapidly to the Kalahari Desert and, finding itself without a proper course, spills over its banks to make an 11-kilometre (7-mile) strip of swampland before spreading out into the Okavango Swamp itself.

The delta in the desert stretches some 241 kilometres (150 miles)

and contains one large island, Chief's Island, as well as other stretches of higher land in which thorn trees and palm trees grow. In the lower-lying swampland the combination of abundant water and sunshine produces giant vegetation. Dense papyrus and reeds grow to 4·57 metres (15 feet) and choke the canals through which the water flows. The plentiful supply of food, including many varieties of fish, attract a large bird population which includes the ibis, stork, egret and crane and provides ideal conditions for hippopotamus and crocodiles.

Plans are now afoot in Botswana, where the swamp lies, to develop a nature reserve, and already at Moremi north of the swamp there is a park with lion, cheetah, buffalo, wildebeeste and zebra.

Far left
The plentiful water and the hot sun have created a botanist's paradise – here is *Nymphaea lotus* one of the many exotic plants that proliferate.
Below left
The water from the Okavango River meanders through dry lands.
Below
There is a rich variety of animal life on the swamp which extends over 16·8 square kilometres (9 square miles). Buffalo and other herbivorous species abound and provide food for predators.

BAALBEK
city of the sun

Once known as Heliopolis, City of the Sun, Baalbek was probably named after Baal, the Lord or Master of the Earth. Set north of Damascus on the route from the western worlds of Greece and Rome to Egypt and Mesopotamia and Persia, it was an important place from the time of the earliest Middle Eastern civilisations. Mark Antony gave Baalbek to Cleopatra, who owned it until she was defeated by Augustus Caesar. He made it a garrison town for his legions and replaced Baal with Jupiter, the chief Roman god.

In subsequent centuries Baalbek suffered from those who took possession of the city. Theodosius destroyed a large part of Jupiter's temple to make way for a basilica, the Saracens transformed it into a citadel during the Crusades, and in the fourteenth century Tamerlane the Great and his army attacked and severely damaged it.

The Germans, who were allies of the Turkish rulers of Lebanon, began the excavation of the temples in 1899. After World War I, Lebanon became a French mandate, and the work of excavation was continued by the French and later by the Lebanese.

The Acropolis of Baalbek contains two important temples, one to Jupiter and one to Bacchus. The Temple of Jupiter is the larger one and was approached through a *propylaea*, or stone entrance, built during the third century AD. This led to a forecourt and then to a large main court 117 metres by 104·5 metres (383 feet by 343 feet) with two altars. There was also a large portico with eighty-four columns of granite brought from Aswan in Egypt, of which only six remain. The Temple of Bacchus is in a

Below and right
The Temple of Bacchus, the best preserved of the buildings at Baalbek. The columns of the Temple are of the Corinthian order.

better condition than that of Jupiter. It is surrounded by a peristyle of columns and has a monumental entrance 12 metres (40 feet) high and 7 metres (23 feet) wide. Originally it was probably dedicated to a youthful local god, and became the Temple of Bacchus during the Roman occupation.

The excavation and rebuilding of Baalbek has revealed the magnitude of the work which the Romans did on the buildings that they found and the magnificence of the town they built on the route to their eastern Empire.

Left
A fragment of the entablature of the Temple of Jupiter. This shows the Greek fret pattern of decoration above which are animal heads.

FACTS ABOUT
BAALBEK

Temple of Jupiter:
88 by 47·5 metres (288 by 156 feet); central cell surrounded by 54 columns 20 metres (66 feet) in height.

Temple of Bacchus:
58 by 36·5 metres (190 by 120 feet) surrounded by 42 columns.

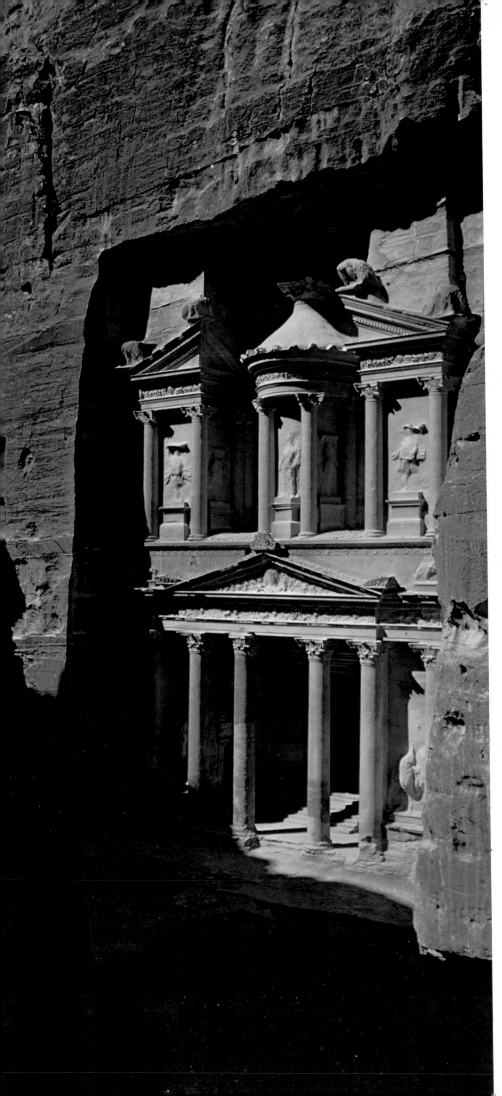

PETRA
a city carved out of rock

Petra in Jordan is almost entirely carved out of its rocky environment – temples, tombs, stairways, theatres emerge out of cliffs in a bewildering virtuoso display of the stone-carver's art. Their colour is unique, for the buildings were carved out of crimson, rose and purple limestone.

How this strange city in its rocky wilderness came to be founded is not yet known, but the people who made it an important centre of early Middle Eastern civilisation were the Nabateans. They were nomadic shepherds who also engaged in the middleman business of carrying the spices of the East to the Mediterranean from where they were shipped to Europe. In the course of time their trading Empire grew until it extended from present-day Syria to Saudi Arabia, and they controlled many of the important caravan routes, becoming wealthy and powerful. They wrested Petra from the Edomites, whose capital it had been in about 300 BC.

In the second century AD the Nabateans were defeated by the Romans, and were incorporated into the Roman Empire, but the importance of Petra as a trading post continued with Roman support. A Roman road was built from Syria to the Red Sea by Trajan, Roman styles in architecture were adopted and Christianity was introduced and replaced the existing worship of the god Dushara.

Only one important building in Petra was built with quarried stone. This was Qasr Firaoun, a vast temple built during the reign of Aretas IV, the great Nabatean king who ruled from 9 BC to AD 40.

Much work is still going on in Petra, the ruins of which were found in 1812. Enough has been discovered to attract thousands of tourists from all over the world, and to establish Petra as one of the wonders of the ancient world.

Far left
The Treasury, built when Hadrian was Emperor of Rome. The sharply sculptured facade has withstood weathering and erosion in this arid area where Moses struck water from the rocks.

Above
The Roman amphitheatre which seated 3,000 people provided entertainment for the troops and merchants who passed through Petra.

Left
The Urn Tomb carved out of rock is nearly all facade. Inside there is only one small room with two even smaller rooms leading into it.

PERSEPOLIS

a palace for King Darius

Darius I was not directly descended from the ruling line of the Achaemenid kings of Persia, so when he ascended to the throne he resolved to start a new style at court. Leaving the original capital at Pasargadae, he built a new palace on a rock 1,747 metres (5,800 feet) above the Persian Gulf at Kuh-i-Rehmat (Mount of Mercy) by the River Araxes.

The work began in 520 BC with grey limestone quarried locally. The main entrance on the west was reached by a double stairway up which horses could climb on ceremonial occasions. At the top of the stairs was a gatehouse guarded by four colossal stone bulls 7 metres (23 feet) high, and an altar. Inscribed on the terrace of the palace were the words: 'I Darius, great king, king of kings, king upon this earth . . . built this fortress.' Darius was the first of a successful line of Persian warrior kings who extended the Persian Empire into the Mediterranean, where they finally came face to face with the redoubtable Athenian Greeks. He was followed by Xerxes, who continued the building of the new city, adding the Gate of all Lands which led to the Apadana, the largest of all the structures at Persepolis. The Apadana was a great hall 60·9 metres (200 feet) square, reached by a staircase decorated with bas-reliefs of guards, 10,000 of them marching along the walls.

Like most buildings of the period, the Apadana strives to impress the onlooker by its size. The columns are 18·8 metres (62 feet) high, and are topped by animals which carry the roof of this great audience chamber.

Under Darius III, Persepolis, with its fabulous treasure of the Achaemenian kings, was lost to Alexander the Great, when the all-conquering Greek overcame the Persians in 331 BC.

Far left
The bull was a symbol of power in ancient times. This winged bull gate was the entrance to the royal palace gardens.
Left
The friezes on the palace walls show soldiers, subject peoples and the daily life of the population of Darius' Empire.
Below
Darius I built an artificial rock-platform on which his palace was erected in 520 BC.

ISPAHAN
city of 200 mosques

Of all the cities of Iran, Ispahan is the one that excites most wonder and admiration. Its great central square, the Maidan, is larger than such famous open spaces as the Piazza in Venice or Trafalgar Square in London, and is bordered by three of the buildings which express the elegance and grace of the architecture of Shah Abbas the Great, who lived from 1587 to 1629.

At the southern end of the Maidan stands the Royal Mosque (Masjid-I-Shah) with its 27·4-metre (90-foot) entrance arch shining with blue tiles set in a stalactite formation. To each side there is a 33·5-metre (110-foot) minaret. The Mosque itself is set at an angle, in line with Mecca, and has a blue tiled court with four portals and a huge dome over the main sanctuary.

On the eastern side is the Lut-fullah Mosque with its tiled portal and dome, which is covered in a complex pattern of tiles. On the other side is Ali Qapu, the entrance to the Royal Palace. This was also a grandstand from which the Shah watched the polo played on the Maidan.

To the north the Maidan leads out to the Bazaars with their narrow alleyways and shops where artisans work on silver and copper.

The tradition of building begun by Shah Abbas was continued by his successors who erected mosques and palaces which still dazzle the eye. One of the most beautiful is the Madraseh-yi-Madar-i-Shah, which was sponsored by the mother of Shah Sultan Hussain as a theological college. It was built in the eighteenth century and has courtyards, gardens, and a dome, all of which have been restored to their former magnificence.

Left
The Sheik Lutfullah Mosque has a
beautiful doorway with stalactite tiles.
The dome has now been restored to its
former beauty.
Right
Reflected in the waters of a pond, the
Sheik Lutfullah Mosque evokes the
colourful image of Turner's Venice.
Below
The college of the Shah's Mother,
Madraseh-yi-Madar-i-Shah, has elegant
minarets each side of its entrance.

JERUSALEM
sacred city of three world religions

For over 3,000 years Jerusalem has been a religious centre torn by internal strife and the prey of foreign invaders. The walls that were built to defend it are still standing, and until 1917, when General Allenby captured the city from the Turks, who had held it since 1244, heavy doors that closed the gates were still in use. The dramatic life story of the city is a measure of the value that different peoples have attached, and still do attach to it.

The most outstanding building in the city is the Dome of the Rock, built by Abd-al-Mali in 691. This stands on the site of a previous Jewish Temple and encloses a sacred stone considered to mark the centre of the world in ancient times, and where Abraham was reputed to have prepared to sacrifice Isaac.

The old city which lies outside the Haran-ash-Sharif, a rectangle of open space where the Temple is situated, consists of tightly packed houses and narrow streets. Among them is a multitude of shrines and

churches of the religions that occupy Jerusalem's Jewish, Moslem, Armenian and Christian quarters. The most important Christian Church is the Holy Sepulchre built by the Emperor Constantine in AD 336 on the site of the crucifixion on Calvary. This was formerly outside the city walls, but as new walls were built it became enclosed in the city itself.

The Church of St Anne occupies the site of the house of the parents of the Virgin Mary and was built in the twelfth century. Between the Haram-ash-Sharif and the Jewish quarter lies the Wailing Wall, and to the north of the centre is the Via Dolorosa, along which Christ walked to his Crucifixion.

One of the oldest buildings in Jerusalem is the Monastery of the Cross; this was built by the mother of the Emperor Constantine on having discovered the True Cross in a cave near the Holy Sepulchre.

Below
The rock on which the famous Dome was built by the Sheik-al-Haram is sacred to Moslems as the spot from which Mahomet departed to heaven; its oldest significance for Christians and Jews is connected with Abraham and also Solomon who built his temple there.

FACTS ABOUT JERUSALEM

Situated in the Judean Hills.
56·32 kilometres (35 miles) from the Mediterranean.
743·7 metres (2,440 feet) above sea level.
Population over $\frac{1}{4}$ million.
Won by Israel in the Six Days' War, 1967.

Above
For Jews, the most sacred spot in Jerusalem is the Wailing Wall, a fragment of Solomon's great temple at which Jewish people pray.
Right
Among the many old churches in Jerusalem is the Coptic Orthodox church.

MOUNT EVEREST

king of mountains

Rising above the other peaks of the Himalayan range in Nepal is Mount Everest, the highest mountain peak in the world. From its stark summit, the snow and ice fall into the rocky valleys below, accumulating as mighty glaciers which inch their way to the warmer levels where they melt and become turbulent streams, feeding the rich growths of bamboo and other subtropical plants along the lower valley.

Khumbu is the glacier in which the base camp for the assault on the top was set up for the successful climb by Edmund Hillary and Tenzing, the Sherpa mountaineer, in 1953. Its valley is the home of the mountain men whose knowledge of the mountain has helped countless climbers to attempt the conquest of the summit.

Everest was recognised as the supreme challenge to climbers in 1852 when its height was recorded and it was named after Sir George Everest, a surveyor. The great series of climbs, undertaken with the most rudimentary equipment, took place between the years 1924 and 1952. On the first of these attempts the climbers Mallory and Irvine disappeared, and the only trace found by a later expedition was their ice axe. The final success of the Royal Geographical Society team led by Sir John Hunt and including Hillary and Tenzing was a triumph of tenacity and daring.

Since then, with all the advantages which modern equipment provides, there have been many successful attempts, including Indian, Japanese, United States and Swiss teams of climbers. Although facing a variety of hazards, none of the climbers has yet met the mysterious Yeti, or 'abominable snowman' who, according to local legend, inhabits the mountain.

Far left
The famous Western Cwm, which has to be tackled when climbing the western face of Everest.
Above
Base camp is nowadays well within reach of most fairly active people including tourists. Pumori is in the background.
Left
Everest has always inspired awe and when the early attempts to climb it failed, there were many who believed that the gods were against such ventures.

THE CAVES OF AJANTA
Buddhist monasteries

Above

Many of the temples have carved exteriors, and this one has several pillars that have been carved out of the rock. Inside there are statues of Buddha, his disciples and female figures.

In central India along a scrub-covered ravine through which a stream flows, there are a series of Buddhist monasteries which provide a remarkable record of a philosophy which has influenced Eastern thought for over two thousand years.

Buddha, the great teacher, who put forward the idea that spiritual peace was only possible by discarding worldly preoccupations, inspired many people to a monastic life. At Ajanta there were about two hundred priests at any one time over a period of several centuries. They dedicated their lives to the principles of Buddhism and carved twenty-nine temples and monasteries out of the rockface.

These carved and decorated caves represent a development of Buddhism which elevated the teacher to the position of a god. This evolution of the religion, known as Mahayana, grew naturally out of the disciples' urge to worship their master. In the early monasteries carved in the second and first centuries BC, god is not represented at all, except by allusion, in the caves, which architecturally are similar to those carved out in Persia at the same or a slightly earlier period. Later the figure of Buddha appears and is shown in the sculptures and paintings.

The carved rock buildings are of two types: the prayer rooms or temples are based on previous wooden structures, and have beams and gables supported on columns, while the monastery residences consist of cells grouped round a central courtyard.

The quality of the architectural carving at Ajanta is of the highest order and the paintings are among the best of Buddhist art in India, giving Ajanta a double claim to be a true wonder of the world.

Above
The Buddhsattva Padmapani fresco is one of the many that decorates the interior of the Caves. The paintings were intended as a means of teaching the facts of Buddha's life to people who were probably illiterate.

THE TAJ MAHAL
for love of Mum Taz

The fifth Mogul Emperor, Shah Jehan, was ruler of northern India in the seventeenth century. During his reign there was a great wave of rebuilding which included Delhi and the Red Fort. His most famous building was the Taj Mahal, erected in memory of his wife Mum Taz. She was his favourite queen and bore him seven children. During her lifetime, she accompanied him on his journeys, sharing in his duties. She was renowned for her charity and compassion.

When Mum Taz died in 1629, Shah Jehan set about building her the most beautiful mausoleum ever conceived. He chose a site by the River Jumna and sank stone foundations and walls over which he built a stone terrace. He planned a garden with canals, stone walls, minarets and a great gate some 30 metres (100 feet) high topped by a half dome and flanked by octagonal turrets.

The mausoleum is basically a square standing on a platform. Each face has a great arch with smaller arches on each side and at each corner of the mausoleum, but separated from it, stand minarets 41·75 metres (137 feet) high. On the roof is a beautiful onion dome topped by a spire and around the dome stand four small turrets with arches. Over all the surfaces there are intricate decorations in lapis lazuli, jasper, agate, heliotrope and turquoise.

When he had completed it, Shah Jehan's intention had been to build a black marble mausoleum on the opposite bank of the river for his own tomb, but destiny decreed otherwise. His son Aurangzeb turned against him and imprisoned him in Agra. He died in 1666 and was laid at his wife's feet in the Taj Mahal.

BOROBUDUR

Buddha's temple

Rising above the palm trees in the countryside near Djakarta, on the Island of Java in the Indonesian Republic, is one of the most exotic temples on earth. Dedicated to Buddha in the eighth century, it embodies many of the ideas which the prophet taught.

The building, more like a stepped hill than a piece of architecture, has five terraces, each standing for one of the steps to the achievement of perfect peace and tranquillity. These, according to Buddha, are the renunciation of earthly desires, of malevolence, malicious joy, indolence and doubt. At the summit of the temple is a platform on which rises an elegant dome with a spire; this represents Nirvana, or the state of complete peace.

Round the main dome are lesser bell-shaped domes, the shape derived from earlier burial mounds, or *stupas*. In the centre of each sits a statue of Buddha.

The lower terraces are extensively decorated with sculpture, including 432 niches, again containing statues of Buddha, while beautifully carved friezes depict scenes from his life. Buddhism arrived in Java after the main tide of the religion had begun to recede on the mainland, and its power did not seem to last long. Two hundred years after the building of the temple at Borobudur it was no longer in use, and the jungle had begun to reclaim

the site on which it stands.

The style of building is one which is found on the mainland, particularly in Cambodia, as developed by the Khmer civilisation in which the temple mountain represented the centre of the universe. It was often associated with the idea of god-kings and became their mausoleum on their death. On the mainland these temples developed from earlier Hindu buildings, but in Borobudur there is no reference to any other religion than Buddhism.

Left
Buddha has many aspects and these are symbolised in the numerous statues carved in the walls of the terraces.

Above
A Buddha and two Buddhsattvas await pilgrims in a temple at Chandi Mendut one of the smaller temples around Borobudur.

Below
There is a profusion of Buddhas at Borobudur and the most important of these sit in lattice-work, bell-shaped 'stupas' in meditation.

ANGKOR WAT

*jungle-held secret of
a past civilisation*

Among the many temples and palaces of the world which tell of a past civilisation, none is more tantalising than Angkor Wat in Cambodia. When discovered by Henri Mouhout, a French naturalist, in 1858, Angkor Wat was buried in the jungle. Over the years clearance of the vegetation has revealed a 48·28-kilometre (30-mile) square area of temples and palaces of the Khmer civilisation.

The Khmer were rulers of what is now Laos, Burma and Vietnam, and were a strong and talented people who between AD 800 and 1200, built an empire, the centre of which was Cambodia. Their kings were earthly monarchs but also divine, and their religion was a form of Hinduism with strong elements of nature worship.

The temple of Angkor Wat was built during the reign of Suryavaram II and dedicated to Vishnu. The whole area is 914·4 metres (3,000 feet) long and surrounded by a wall with five towers. The temple itself rises in terraces covered with smaller temples and represents the centre of the universe. Thousands of sculptures decorate the alleyways between the shrines on every terrace, and above them all rises the pinnacle of the temple.

Nearby are the remains of the city of Angkor Thom, the old capital of the Khmers. Three hundred years after the building of the latter, the whole area was deserted, and the jungle and wild animals took over. The reason for this mass desertion remains a mystery, perhaps to be solved by future archaeologists.

Far left
The inner sanctuary of Bantey Srei (Citadel of the Women) was dedicated in AD 968.
Left. Huge heads of Buddha stare impassively from the towers, but he shares his kingdom with the Hindu gods, Vishnu and Shiva who were venerated by other rulers.
Below
There are thirty buildings in the vicinity of Angkor Wat. Although now clear of vegetation, it is still the home of monkeys', toucans and other exotic flora and fauna.

FACTS ABOUT
ANGKOR WAT

Area of complex:
1,303 by 1,499 metres (1,425 by 1,640 yards).
Outer enclosure of temple:
187·45 by 214·88 metres (205 by 235 yards).
First platform:
13·7 metres (45 feet) high.
Central tower:
65·5 metres (215 feet) high.

SHWE DAGON

the golden pagoda

No one knows exactly when Shwe Dagon, the tallest religious building in the world, which stands near Rangoon, was built. It is known to have evolved from the burial mounds, or *stupas*, in which Buddhists inter their dead, and there is evidence of Shwe Dagon having been repaired in 1362, so it is at least six hundred years old.

During its life it has had numerous additions and alterations, one of the most important of which was during the reign of King Mindon Min, who in 1871 spent

£4·5 million, covering the main dome in gold. The spire of the pagoda, which was once studded with real emeralds, rubies, diamonds and other precious stones, was added in the eighteenth century.

Today, the Shwe Dagon, which rises in a pure golden shape from its base, is as much a popular centre of pilgrimage as ever. Its sacred character is enhanced by the possession of eight of Buddha's hairs which according to legend were brought there by two brothers, Tapusa and Palikat. Pilgrims come to hear the preachers who set themselves up by the shrines which surround the central pagoda. They may even contribute to the pagoda's appearance by sticking on bits of gold leaf.

The pagoda stands on a 55-metre (180-foot) high mound and covers 62,709 square metres (75,000 square yards). The corners are guarded by Nats (tree and river spirits) and dragons, and other beasts guard the shrines around the base.

Above left
The great golden shrine of Shwe Dagon rises 98 metres (321 feet) into the sky from a base 433 metres (1,420 feet) in circumference.
Far left
Picturesque lions guard the sacred precinct of the pagoda against evil spirits.
Above
Around the base of Shwe Dagon are colourful shrines with gilded spires.

THE HÔRYÛ-JI
a treasury of Buddhist art

Near Nara in Japan lies the Hôryû-ji, the oldest Buddhist temple in the country. It dates back to the seventh century and is a fantastic treasure trove of Buddhist art. Its Main Hall, or Kondô, is perhaps the oldest wooden building in the world, and there are other buildings of great architectural significance in the temple complex.

Among these is the five-storeyed Pagoda, which is 31·7 metres (105 feet) in height and possesses a series of tableaux of clay-sculptured figures representing scenes from Buddhist history. One of these shows the Nirvana of Buddha.

The Kondô stands to the east of the Pagoda. It is a two-storeyed building with a fine roof with carved eaves and columns. In the simple interior there are bronze statues including the Shaka Triad and the Buddha of Healing.

Other buildings in the complex include a Lecture Hall of a later date and the Kyozo or Sutra depository where the complete set of Buddhist scriptures are stored. The great treasures of the Hôryû-ji are preserved in a modern concrete building in which statues and manuscripts, threatened over the years by a series of fires, are now in safe keeping.

The eastern area of Hôryû-ji consists of more modern buildings, though there is an eighth-century Hall of Dreams which is built on the site of the palace of Prince Shotoku, founder of the Hôryû-ji. There is also a Preaching Hall which was originally built as a residence for one of the lady members of the Emperor's court.

Far left
Despite the vast spread of its many roofs the tall pagoda of Hôryû-ji is so perfectly proportioned that it retains its sense of height.
Above
The Kondo hall is the oldest wooden building in the world. It was built in AD 607 when Europe was in the Dark Ages.
Left
One of the most valuable treasures of Hôryû-ji is the Buddha Sakyamuni, a triad of three figures in gilded bronze.

THE GREAT WALL OF CHINA
longest defence system in the world

A great wall running 2,414 kilometres (1,500 miles) from the Gulf of Chihli into Central Asia over difficult mountain terrain was the main defence of the ancient Chinese against invasions by northern tribes. The first wall was begun by Chin Shih Huang Ti in the third century BC. He linked together existing sections of wall to create a more continuous system of defence against the Hsiung-nu, a wild tribe of horse-riding nomads known in Europe as the Huns.

To speed up the building of the wall, hundreds of thousands of

Below
From the vantage point of the Wall, which varies in height from 6–15 metres (20–50 feet), soldiers watched for nomadic tribes.
Inset
A relief panel from the Tüan dynasty inside Chii-yung Gate.
Right
The Wall, which is 3,219 kilometres (2,000 miles) long, meanders through wild and inhospitable mountains which provide perfect terrain for guerilla warfare.

workmen and even released criminals were set to the task. Even this vast labour force was not enough to complete it during Chin Shih's lifetime. A twenty-four hour vigil defended the wall and a system of smoke signals was devised to warn of attack on any one section of the wall.

In the fourteenth century a plan for another wall some 16,093 kilometres (10,000 miles) long was made by the Ming Emperors, who were now threatened by the Mongol tribes led by Genghis Khan.

The Ming Emperors, whose tombs line the famous avenue to the mausoleums outside Peking, retained the same architectural techniques as Chin Shih and built brick walls on a stone foundation, filling in the centre with gravel, bricks and clay. A watchtower in which guards were stationed was erected every 150 metres (492 feet), and there was a roadway providing swift communication.

Despite the wall the north of China has always been a vulnerable spot, and even today an army is kept at this frontier.

**FACTS ABOUT
THE GREAT WALL OF
CHINA**

Total length:
3,219 kilometres (2,000 miles), including branches and windings.
Height:
6–15 metres (20–50 feet).
Width:
4·5–7·6 metres (15–25 feet).
Towers:
9 metres (30 feet) high, 6 metres (20 feet) wide.
Begun 204 BC.

PEKING
the Forbidden City

Top
From Prospect Hill there is a panoramic view of the City which is 1·6 by 2·4 kilometres (1 by 1½ miles) in area. Tian-an-Men Square outside the South Wall is 40·5 hectares (100 acres) in size and is a gathering place on great occasions.
Above
The Vault of Heaven was built during the Ming period and is similar in appearance to the Hall of Prayers.

Eighty kilometres (50 miles) south of the Great Wall of China lies the Forbidden City, first built by the all-conquering Kublai Khan about whom Coleridge wrote, 'In Xanadu did Kublai Khan a stately pleasure dome decree . . .' But Kublai Khan's pleasure dome was not the one that lives on today; this was planned by Yung Lo in the fifteenth century, two hundred years after the Mongol Emperor. The city within which the Forbidden City stands is a vast 64·75 square-kilometre (25 square-mile) rectangle of buildings and gardens enclosed by walls and divided into the Outer and Inner City.

The true Forbidden City lies in the Inner City whose main entrance is known as the Gate of Heavenly Peace. Before this gate is a vast square used for parades and reviews and a moat crossed by five marble bridges. In Im-perial times, the Emperor, accompanied by two parallel processions on each side, would enter the City over the central bridge. The five parallel avenues lead into the City through a courtyard and a second gate, to reach the huge gate of the Meridian. Beyond this lies another courtyard crossed by the Golden River, and then the Gate of Supreme Harmony, leading to the Hall of the same name where the Imperial throne stood. This is the heart of the Forbidden City, and only the Emperor and his closest attendants penetrated it.

On the triple terrace on which the Hall stands are eighteen bronze incense burners, a huge dragon-headed tortoise and a stone sundial. On each side of the Hall are audience halls. It was in the midst of these impressive surroundings that the Emperor, ruler of the world by divine mandate,

received homage from his princes.

The grandeur of the concept of the Imperial City can be appreciated from Prospect Hill, to the north of the City; and from here the sloping roofs of yellow tiles, the towers, palaces and temples can be seen in one sweep.

In the Outer City, a rectangular area to the south adjoining the Inner City, lies the Altar of Heaven, where only the Emperor could make offerings to Heaven as its only true representative on earth. The Altar is, in fact, a large walled area with a number of temples, the most important of which is the Temple of Heaven, an elegant circular tower with three roofs encircling it at intervals of its 27·43-metre (90-foot) rise. Services at the Temple of Heaven took place rarely, and always in the Emperor's presence.

FACTS ABOUT
PEKING

City:
64·75 square kilometres (25 square miles).
Imperial City:
1·6 by 2·4 kilometres (1 by 1½ miles).
Hall of Supreme Harmony:
64 by 35 metres (210 by 115 feet).
Tian-an-Men Square, outside southern wall of Forbidden City, 40·46 hectares (100 acres) in area.

Above
The Gate of Supreme Harmony, one of the main City gates which now houses the National Museum with its superb collection of jewellery, ceramics and costumes.
Right
The Hall of Prayers lies in the centre of the Temple of Heaven complex.

THE FORT AT LAHORE
key to the Punjab

Right
Mosaics reflect the love of nature of Lahore's rulers.

Lahore was an important key point controlling the rich grain lands of the Punjab even before the Mogul Emperor Babur arrived in 1524. Under the Mogul Empire, it grew both in extent and in beauty. The main contributors to the new Lahore were the Emperors Akbar and Shah Jehan. The former, who reigned from 1556 to 1605, rebuilt the city walls and the citadel which, in succeeding generations, was to become the great fort of Lahore.

In the walls of the fort, Akbar erected the Masti Gate, a massive construction with battlements protecting the east side of the fort.

Akbar's son, Jahangir, continued his father's work with a quadrangle, cloisters and other buildings. His own interest in nature resulted in the paintings of the flora and fauna of the region which decorate the Diwan-i-Amm, or Hall of General Audience.

Shah Jehan, builder of the Taj Mahal, also dedicated part of the Lahore Fort to his Empress. This was the Palace of Glass, built in 1632, and so called because of the glass used in the inlaid mosaic decorations. Shah Jehan also erected a number of marble buildings, including the Diwan-i-Mas, or Special Audience Hall, and the lovely Pearl Mosque. In the final days of the Mogul Empire the Emperor Aurangzeb added further buildings to the fort, including the monumental western Alamgiri gate, and a superb mosque, the Badshahi (Imperial) Mosque, immediately outside the fort walls.

The Sikhs, who followed the Mogul Emperors as rulers of Lahore, made their own contributions to this splendid fort which with its exquisite tiled walls and floors and inlaid walls, has been restored to become one of the most beautiful complex of buildings in the world.

Below
There were three phases in the building of the Lahore Fort. Akbar's Fort started in the sixteenth century covered 1,570 square metres (16,800 square feet) which was added to by Shah Jehan and Aurangzeb in the seventeenth century.

HONG KONG
an exotic beehive

Hong Kong Island and Kowloon, across the bay on the mainland, cover only 85·47 square kilometres (33 square miles), but most of the Colony's population of over four million live there. The result is that urban Hong Kong is a closely packed complex of high-rise buildings with ever-crowded streets. However, this was not always the case.

When the Western powers first began seeking trade with China, Hong Kong was almost unpopulated. Trading permission was granted only in Canton by the Manchu Emperor who regarded all foreigners as barbarians. He may have been right, for the Westerners began to smuggle opium into China and this soon became a national addiction. The attempt to stop this traffic led to the Opium War between China and Britain, and the Treaty of Nanking which ended the War in

Far left
In busy Cat Street there are many curio shops. This area of Hong Kong island has open-fronted shops and stalls which sell all manner of exotic products.
Left
The sampan dwellers at Aberdeen Harbour are some of the 5 per cent of the Hong Kong population that live in floating houses.
Below
At Tiger Balm Garden there are displays of Chinese folklore in Disneyesque style.

FACTS ABOUT HONG KONG

Population:
  over 5 million.
Main areas:
  Hong Kong Island, Kowloon, New Territories, outer islands (200).
Occupied by British 1839.
Ceded to Britain by Treaty of Nanking, 1842.
Kowloon Peninsula ceded to Britain 1860.
New territories due to be returned to China on July 1, 1998.

1842 gave the British Hong Kong.

The island grew into an import–export centre of the East, and in recent years has become one of the most important industrial regions in Asia. Hong Kong is made up of Hong Kong Island, Kowloon and the New Territories on the mainland, the latter being leased to Britain by the Chinese until 1998. The terrain is very mountainous, which aggravates the problems of overcrowding. But it is perhaps this very condition that has made Hong Kong such a unique place – the will to survive has created a teeming, industrious community which has developed a colourful and contrasted life. Skyscrapers and sophisticated hotels rub shoulders with crowded tenements, gleaming modern cars are jostled by bicycles and rickshaws, glossy shops compete with street markets.

CHICHEN ITZÁ
relic of a cruel civilisation

The Castillo or castle. The Temple of Kukulcan was connected to the sacrificial well by a road down which the victims marched to their death.

The Maya Indians of Mexico, descendants of early peoples who crossed to the Americas from Asia via the Bering Strait, developed a culture in which barbaric cruelty and high intellectual attainments existed side by side.

On the one hand the Mayas practised human sacrifice, cutting out the hearts of their living victims to offer to their god. On the other, they developed the science of astronomy, the arts of architecture and hieroglyphic writing and discovered the mathematical value of the number zero. Strangely enough, however, they never invented the wheel.

The centre of this civilisation was Chichen Itzá in the Yucatan peninsula. The discoverer of its treasure was Thompson, an American who spent his life unravelling the secrets of the Mayas.

Chichen Itzá was one of the later additions to the many temples which the Mayas erected to their savage gods. It consists of a complex of buildings covering an area of 3·2 by 2 kilometres (2 by $1\frac{1}{4}$ miles). The largest building is the Temple of Warriors, a twelfth-century edifice built over the older temple of Chacmool. In the centre lies the Castillo, a raised building in direct line from which is the Well of Sacrifice, where young girls were once thrown to

propitiate the gods.

A feature of Chichen Itzá is the colonnades which surround the squares and the great market, Mercado, which may have played a similar role for the Mayas to that of the Roman Forum as a gathering place for the populace.

It is very probable that the Mayas were originally a tranquil, nature-worshipping people who acquired their violent religious rituals after conquest by the Toltec tribes of central Mexico. In the end, however, they succumbed to a greater violence than their own when the Conquistadors arrived hungering for the gold and other Mayan treasures.

The jaguar heads give this temple its name. The carvings depict the story of the Toltec conquest and a description of the rites which involved human sacrifice.

Right
The temple of the Warriors has roof supports shaped like plumed serpents, a Toltec symbol. This view is from the Pyramid of Kukulcan.

FACTS ABOUT
CHICHEN ITZÁ

115·8 kilometres (72 miles) south-east of Merida, Yucatan, Mexico.
Total area, about 2 by 3·2 kilometres (1¼ by 2 miles) long.
Well of Sacrifice:
    48·8 metres (160 feet) in diameter.
    21 metres (70 feet) from lip to water.
Ball Court:
    92 by 7·6 metres (270 by 25 feet).

THE GRAND CANYON
Nature's masterpiece

There is no record of what Francisco Garces and Silvestri Velez de Escalante said when they first saw the Grand Canyon in the course of their explorations of the Colorado River in 1776. Perhaps this is because they were stunned into silence by the extraordinary spectacle.

The Grand Canyon was dug out of the Colorado plateau by the Colorado River, which eroded the Mesozoic rocks of 225 million years ago and then worked its way down through the granite and schist of the lower strata. The astonishing formation of the Canyon is due to the dry climate of the region and the consequent lack of weathering of the Canyon sides.

The Canyon extends from Marble Gorge to Grand Wash Cliffs, but its most spectacular area is contained in the Grand Canyon National Park, a section of some 169 kilometres (105 miles), declared a park area in 1919.

The erosion by the river has laid bare millions of years of the earth's strata, and thereby provided geologists with perfect terrain for their research. Evidence of primitive creatures and early man has been discovered as well as more recent relics of the habitations of rock-dwelling people and the Pueblo Indians.

In the area are also such spectacular natural wonders as Monument Valley, whose sheer pillars of rock have been the scene for many a western film, and the Painted Desert.

Over two million visitors arrive at this wonder of the world every year. They trek by mule and horse around the dizzy precipices, or raft down the Colorado River to experience for themselves some of the awe which the first explorers of the area felt.

Left
Way below the sheer canyon walls, the Colorado River winds its way to the sea. The deepest canyon is 1·6 kilometres (1 mile).
Above
The Grand Canyon stretches from Marble Gorge to Grand Wash Cliffs; approximately 450·5 kilometres (280 miles) of breathtaking scenery.

FACTS ABOUT
THE GRAND CANYON

Length from Marble Gorge to Grand Wash Cliffs, approximately 450 kilometres (280 miles).
Width:
6·4–29 kilometres (4–18 miles).
Depth:
in places, more than 1·6 kilometres (1 mile).

THE NIAGARA FALLS
America's great natural spectacle

Honeymoon haven, holiday resort and marvel of nature, the Niagara Falls between the United States and Canada, although not the largest or longest falls in the world, have attracted more spectators than almost any other natural wonder in the world. Over the years, tourist facilities have grown rapidly, ensuring that visitors can enjoy the Falls from every possible angle, and today they can be seen from the top of two towers, from a bridge, from below, from pleasure steamers and from helicopters. They are also floodlit so that spectators can enjoy them by night as well as by day.

About ten thousand years ago during the Pleistocene Age, the Niagara River began to flow as the ice from the sheet that covered North America began to melt. The River flowed from what is today Lake Erie to Lake Ontario. Halfway along its course over hard Dolomitic rock it came across a softer strata and began to erode it away. This process

Above
The Horseshoe Fall which provides the greatest spectacle of Niagara is on the Canadian side and is three times as wide as the American Fall.

FACTS ABOUT
THE NIAGARA FALLS

Horseshoe Fall:
  48 metres (158 feet) high.
  792·5 metres (2,600 feet) wide.
American Fall:
  51 metres (167 feet) high.
  305 metres (1,000 feet) wide.
Rainbow Bridge spans 305-metre (1,000-foot) gorge.
About 94% of the water passes over Horseshoe Fall, the rest over American Fall.

led to the Falls as they were discovered by early settlers, but present fears are that the continuing erosion may diminish the spectacle which they provide. Already, some shoring up of the American Fall has been carried out.

The Falls are in two parts separated by Goat Island. On the Canadian bank is the Horseshoe Fall, and on the opposite bank the American Fall. The water pours down into a navigable area known as the Maid of the Mist Pool on the Canadian side, and then there is a further drop of 28 metres (93 feet) to the Whirlpool Rapids. The water from both Falls eventually flows away through the 11-kilometre (7-mile) long Niagara Gorge.

Left
A close-up view of the Horseshoe Fall.
Right
The American Fall, 305 metres (1,000 feet) wide, sometimes provides a different kind of wonder when it freezes in winter.

MANHATTAN
New York's striking skyline

The skyline of Manhattan, the island on which the city of New York is built, is the most spectacular urban silhouette ever seen. Passengers travelling across the Hudson River are greeted by a solid wall of tall buildings with even higher towers rising above them, a sight which leaves an indelible impression.

In 1524, when the island was first sighted by the navigator Verrazano, it was so unimpressive that he did not bother to stop. It was the Dutch who first settled there, and gave it the name of New Amsterdam. In 1664 they lost this to the British, who re-named it New York after James, Duke of York, upon whom Charles II had bestowed the New World rights.

The early settlers lived on what is the tip of the island (now called the Battery). Here is the business end of New York, where the buildings of Wall Street and the skyscrapers of the New York Telephone Company, the Irving Trust Company, First National Bank, Chase Manhattan Bank (244 metres [800 feet] high) and other business houses look across Hudson Bay to the Statue of Liberty on Bedloe Island.

Between lower Manhattan and the business quarter lie the Villages, where immigrants have settled, giving their new environment their own ethnic characteristics. Here is Chinatown, Little Italy, and the East Side – with a predominant Puerto Rican and Jewish population.

In mid-town, towards Central Park, there are more skyscrapers. The famous Empire State Building still has one of the best viewpoints, though it can no longer claim the title of the tallest building, which now belongs to the 110-storey World Trade Centre. The Woolworth Building is an

American version of the Gothic style, and towers 244 metres (800 feet) over the pavements below, while the monolithic United Nations rises 165·7 metres (544 feet) over the Hudson River.

Another famous skyscraper immediately recognisable by its elegant spire is the Chrysler building, 319·5 metres (1,048 feet) high. This was the first building in which stainless steel was used. Amongst the giants are others which, anywhere but in New York, would also merit the name skyscraper, but here they are merely the supporting cast to the stars of the architectural firmament.

Left
From downtown New York there is a spectacular view of Manhattan and the East River totalling an area of 56·9 square kilometres (22 square miles). The area is bounded by New York Bay, Hudson River, Spuyten Dayvil Creek, Harlem River and East River.

Inset above
Night-time in New York and the skyscrapers light up like Christmas trees.
Inset below
The skyline with Brooklyn Bridge; the tall monolith on the right is the World Trade Centre.

LAS VEGAS

the gamblers heaven

Roulette, blackjack, chemin de fer, poker, craps and almost every other form of gambling ever conceived by man are available at Las Vegas, Nevada's biggest city, and the over four million people who visit it every year are regaled with entertainments that feature the most famous artistes in the world. In addition, Las Vegas is one of the world's biggest marriage factories, with 500 people licensed to tie the bonds instantly for those who want to dispense with the fuss and bother of the ritual in other states.

Boisterous and colourful, Las Vegas was once nothing but a wayside stop set up by the Spaniards in a green patch 2,162 feet above sea level and surrounded by 3,352-metre (11,000-foot) mountains, in an arid landscape. This gave it its name; Las Vegas means 'The Meadows'.

The Mormons went through it in their pioneering journey to the west when they founded Salt Lake City, and later the Union Pacific Railway arrived. Las Vegas was also a prospector's town when silver was discovered in the neighbourhood. It was not until it became the headquarters of the world's largest gambling enterprises that Las Vegas really struck it rich. By 1960 the population had grown several times and today it is up to nearly 300,000. Among those who have helped to develop the gambling and entertainment facilities of the city are men like the famous Howard Hughes and Kirk Kirkorian, who also controls MGM. The town has not been short of colourful characters, such as Nick the Greek, who is reputed to have spent 50 million dollars at the tables.

The main part of Las Vegas is known as The Strip. This is the entertainment, hotel and gambling palace boulevard where fluorescent signs turn the night into day. Another area is Downtown, and there is a large Convention Centre where business conferences take place. Near Las Vegas are Boulder Dam, Lake Mead, Death Valley and the ghost towns where the former silver seekers lived.

Below
In some ways the Strip is just another American main street but the ostentatious signs like this one, inviting you to the 'Frontier', reveal its true identity.

Left
Although Las Vegas is a show that goes on night and day, the neon signs come into their own when the sun goes down.

Inset
The famous Golden Nugget reminds customers of the old days of gold-mining bonanzas and the sign on the left promises to give away 250,000 dollars.

Bottom
The Mint; wherever you look in Las Vegas the promise is easy money.

DISNEY WORLD
the most amazing fantasy factory in history

The Walt Disney World in Florida, USA, is the most amazing concentration of fantasy worlds ever assembled in the history of man. Disney World is not one but six worlds, each one of which·has proved, through the mass medias of the cinema and television, to have universal appeal.

The whole of the Disney World occupies 111·36 square kilometres (43 square miles), and includes hotels, camping grounds, golf courses and lakes. The centre of it all is the Magic Kingdom.

This is divided into various main themes: Main Street is a world of the recent past, what most people think of nostalgically as the 'good old days'. Here in the Disney World Main Street are all the romantic and picturesque items of the Victorian and Edwardian epoch. Horseless carriages, vintage cars, old fire engines, a singing barber-shop and a Victorian restaurant.

In Adventure Land there are all the famous heroes and villains of an adventurous past. Scenes from the days of the buccaneers of the Caribbean are brought to life, as are the frontier days in America. Traders of Timbuktu recreates the days of trading in Africa and a Jungle Cruise takes the passengers through crocodile-infected swamps and river banks crowded with wild life.

Another world is based on the theme of famous stories, many of them the subject of Walt Disney films; there is Snow White and the Seven Dwarfs, Tom Sawyer, Dumbo, the Swiss Family Island Treehouse, Toad of Toad Hall and many others.

The future is another fruitful theme, with Starjets, Missions to Mars and Space Mountain providing all the thrills of an imaginary future world.

For most of the twelve million people who visit Disney World every year, the most impressive feature is the size and perfection of the exhibits. In the Hall of Presidents, all the Presidents of the United States are presented in Audioanimatronics, a system of animation which enables a model of such as President Lincoln to rise and make a speech and move in a realistic manner.

This kind of fantasy, which is almost indistinguishable from reality, is the real wonder of Disney World, and makes it a type of entertainment unique in the history of man.

Above left
The Disney World fairy castle is not unlike Neuschwanstein.
Left
Rudyard Kipling's Jungle Book characters in Disney style.

Above
Getting around the world of Disney is made easy by modern monorail. All photographs © Walt Disney Productions.

MOUNT PALOMAR

looking into a billion light years of space

In a white-domed observatory over 1,707 metres (5,600 feet) up Mount Palomar in California, man has been trying to solve the riddle of space since the giant Hale telescope was installed there in 1947.

This giant telescope takes in 360,000 times as much light as the human eye, and has enabled man to photograph objects in space billions of light years away. Since a light year is the distance that light can travel in a year, that is 9·5 trillion kilometres (6 trillion miles) the depths of space explored by the telescope are almost impossible to visualise.

With this powerful and sensitive instrument many famous astronomers have discovered new facts about the universe. Albert A. Michelson worked out how to measure the diameter of stars, and Edwin Hubble developed his provocative theory that the universe is in a period of expansion which makes all the objects in it appear to be receding from each other at enormous speeds.

The largest telescope on Earth was named after George Hale, a distinguished astronomer who was director of another famous observatory, Mount Wilson. He was the discoverer of the effect of sunspots on magnetic fields on Earth.

The Hale telescope is not Palomar's only instrument capable of widening man's knowledge of the space his world floats in. There is also a Schmidt telescope there. This maps out and locates bodies in the sky, and covers an area of sky 800 times greater than the Hale is capable of. This facilitates a more rapid search of the vast expanse of space. It took seven years to map out the skies of the northern hemisphere and half of the southern.

The work of the Palomar observatory is a reminder that, despite the achievements of extraterrestrial travellers, most of space is a vast unknown lying far outside the reach of any journey that could be accomplished in one person's entire life.

Left
The 41-metre (134-foot) Mount Palomar observatory building is seen here at night at the start of operation.
Above
The 508-centimetre (200-inch) mirror enables man to see further into space than ever before.
Right
The precision of the focussing mechanism helps to pinpoint universes many light years distant.

EASTER ISLAND

remnant of a sunken continent?

FACTS ABOUT
EASTER ISLAND

3,218·68 kilometres (2,000 miles) from Caldera, Chile; 1,769·9 kilometres (1,100 miles) from Pitcairn.
Extent 17·7 by 24·14 kilometres (11 by 15 miles).
Highest volcanic mountain, 537·9 metres (1,765 feet).

Two thousand miles (3,218 kilometres) from the coast of northern Chile in the south Pacific Ocean lies volcanic Easter Island, with its giant carved heads gazing impassively into space, and revealing nothing about their origins or purpose.

Despite opinions to the contrary, to most people the myth that Easter Island is the remnant of a large continent which sank below the waves will always be credible. It is easy to imagine a doomed people filling the island with figures to propitiate the gods and carving effigies of themselves with gaunt faces and protruding ribs as the islands on which they grew their food disappeared below the sea.

Modern anthropologists believe, however, that the Easter Islanders were simply a decadent Polynesian people who just faded away. The island, also called Rapa Nui, was discovered by a Dutch Admiral, Jacob Roggeveen, on Easter Sunday 1722. In 1888 it was annexed by Chile and

Far left
Many of the statues on Easter Island were placed with their backs to the sea but these stare out towards the horizon as if waiting for help.
Below
The large simply-carved forms of the heads made of volcanic 'tufa' may represent dead ancestors.

its name was translated into Spanish as Isla de Pascua. Since leprosy was endemic among the islanders, the Chileans confined them to one part of the island and set up cattle and sheep stations on the rest.

The statues which give rise to speculations about their creators measure from 3·5 to 6 metres (12 to 20 feet) in height, and some of them appear to be wearing top hats another 1·8 metres (6 feet) high. They are made of a kind of volcanic rock called tufa, and stand on stone platforms. Apart from the statues, little else has been found on the island; there are no metal objects or pottery.

According to one island legend, there was a war between the long- and short-eared men which may have led to the collapse of whatever society the islanders had created. There is little evidence to go on, however, and the mystery of remote Easter Island and its strange uncommunicative statues will continue to give rise to investigations and new theories.

THE GALÁPAGOS ISLANDS
living proof of the theory of evolution

By a strange quirk of circumstance the isolated Galápagos Islands provided Charles Darwin with the final nudge he needed towards formulating his theories on evolution. The islands are volcanic and lie in the Pacific on the Equator 965·6 kilometres (600 miles) west of Ecuador. Naturalists believe the fauna originated on the mainland, but because of contrary winds and currents remained trapped on the islands, where they developed characteristics different from the original species.

Darwin's revolutionary theory that all species on earth had evolved and were not the same as on the day of Creation seemed proved by the fauna of the Galápagos. When he visited the Islands in 1835 he very soon saw how animals and birds on the Galápagos had changed owing to the local environmental pressures. The birds now called Darwin finches, for example, had developed from one ancestor into a variety of species with differing characteristics suitable to their survival needs. Other animals that had adapted to the local environment were the iguanas, the giant tortoises, now extinct elsewhere, and the flightless cormorant.

The Galápagos were dis-covered in 1535 and settled in 1832. They rise from 2,133·6 to 3,048 metres (7,000 to 10,000 feet) above sea level. There are sixteen islands in the archipelago, many of them with large craters. Fernandina's crater is 3·21 by 7 kilometres (2 by 4·5 miles) across, and the largest, Volcan Sierra Negra, is 6.43 by 9·65 kilometres (4 by 6 miles) across.

Inhabitants on the islands have raised goats and cattle, but many of these have gone wild. Despite the islands' remoteness, twentieth-century interest in evolution has ensured the inhabitants an income from tourism.

Above left
The Giant Tortoise is a disappearing
species but in the Galápagos they are
protected.
Above
These rocky and solitary islands offered
no treasures to early sailors and were
thus left undisturbed.
Right
The Marine Iguana gave rise to stories
of dragons and are perhaps descendants
of giant prehistoric reptiles.

MACHU PICCHU
last redoubt of the Inca Empire

The story of the conquest of the Inca Empire in South America by Francisco Pizarro and a handful of Spanish adventurers is one of dissension and greed. In 1532 rivalry and quarrelling among the Indians gave Pizarro the opportunity he needed to capture the Inca chief Atahualpa and plunder the gold and treasure of the Inca Empire. But his triumph was short-lived. Fighting broke out among the Spanish adventurers, and Pizarro and many of his followers were killed. The Indians attempted counter-attacks against the Spaniards from mountain strongholds, of which Machu Picchu near Cuzco, in an almost inaccessible situation on a peak surrounded by 304·8-metre (1,000-foot) high cliffs, was probably one.

When Hiram Bingham, an American explorer, discovered Machu Picchu in 1911, the jungle had overgrown it and there was little left except ruined buildings. These proved to be superb examples of the Inca skills in archi-

tecture: temples and shrines, stone water basins and thousands of stone stairways leading to the various terraces of the mountain city.

In Machu Picchu there is surprisingly little evidence of human habitation: no statues, altars, or domestic artefacts such as are found in buried cities a good deal older. Was this because the stronghold had been discovered and plundered? The fate of Machu Picchu is a mystery which may never be solved.

After the Inca revolt, a puppet ruler, Manco Capac, was set up, but under Manco II the Indians once again began a guerrilla war against the Spaniards from their mountain hideouts. Manco was pursued by the Spanish armies and caught and killed; he was the last of the Incas. If he was attempting to escape to his secret city of Machu Picchu when captured it could be that the Spaniards did discover its whereabouts. If they did, they kept their secret well.

Left
The 40 hectares (100 acres) of buildings at Machu Picchu are surrounded by terraces on which the Incas raised corn, tomatoes and potatoes.
Above
The Temple of the Sun. The Incas worshipped the sun and knew much about its movements. They had not developed a system of writing but messages were recorded through knotted strings.

FACTS ABOUT
MACHU PICCHU

80·4 kilometres (50 miles) north-west of Cuzco, Peru.
2,057 metres (6,750 feet) above sea-level.
609 metres (2,000 feet) above Urubamba River.
Discovered by Hiram Bingham in 1911.

THE IGUAZU FALLS
the great waters of South America

Above
The horseshoe-shaped Falls, consisting
of twenty-one separate falls, plunge
60·5 metres (200 feet) into the valley
below.
Right
The volume of water increased by heavy
equatorial rainfall crashes over the
abyss and sends up a plume of spray.

The Guarani tribes which inhabit the southern borders of Brazil and Paraguay where they meet the Argentinian Republic call the Falls on the Iguazu River the 'great waters' for a good reason. The heavy tropical rainfall of the area drains away to the Iguazu River, which pours over the edge of the Parana Plateau at the rate of roughly 130,000 cubic metres (4,500,000 cubic feet) per second during the rainy season.

The Falls were discovered by a Spanish conquistador with the resounding name of Alvar Nunez Cabeza de Vaca (literal translation: 'A. N. Head of a Cow') who named them Salto de Santa Maria. The first investigation and records of the Falls were made by Jesuit missionaries who settled in the area and were so successful in educating and improving the lives of the Indians that they attracted less scrupulous pioneers who exploited the Guarani, sold them into slavery and caused the Jesuits to be expelled from their missions in 1767.

At the Falls, the river spills over a huge horseshoe crescent into a gorge 60 to 80 metres (197 to 262·4 feet) below. The cliff is broken by outcrops on which the streams of water dash themselves, flinging up great clouds of spray which rise up to 152·4 metres (500 feet) and produce a remarkable variety of rainbows. At Garganta del Diablo, or Devil's Throat, the gorge below the Falls, the span of the largest rainbow is 119 metres (390 feet).

Above the Falls are two large islands, the Isla San Martin, named after the liberator of South America from Spanish domination, and the Isla Grande, as well as lesser islands. Because of their remote situation the Falls have not become industrialised or commercialised, and their beauty and the National Park founded there by Edmundo de Barros in 1897 attract two million tourists each year.

RIO DE JANEIRO
most spectacular harbour in the world

On Guanabara Bay, enveloped by a range of mountains covered with tropical vegetation and inhabited by many species of wild animals and exotic birds, lies a city of skyscrapers of advanced design which provide a stimulating contrast to their dramatic setting.

Rio de Janeiro, which was discovered in 1504 by Gonzalo Coelho, or possibly by Andre Goncalves and Amerigo Vespucci, the man who gave his name to the Americas, was first settled by the French but later captured by the Portuguese. Until 1960 it was the capital of Brazil, after

Left
From the cable car up 395 metres (1,296 feet) to the Sugar Loaf Mountain there is a bird's-eye view of the wonders of Rio de Janeiro.
Inset
The famous Sugar Loaf Mountain at the entrance to the harbour of Rio de Janeiro is visible in the distance in this view towards Nictheroy.
Below
From above the Corcovado mountain, 704 metres (2,310 feet) high, there is a view of the Christ of Corcovado and the Sugar Loaf mountain beyond.

Carioca cuts through the middle of the city, the two parts of which are connected by the longest urban tunnel in the world. The mountains culminate in a sheer conical peak named the Sugar Loaf, a famous landmark. It is 395 metres (1,296 feet) above sea-level, and the top is accessible by cable car. Another remarkable peak in the same range is Corcovado, the Hunchbank. This is 704 metres (2,309·7 feet) above sea-level, and on its summit stands a colossal statue of Christ the Redeemer, completed in 1931.

To the south of Rio de Janeiro lies Gavea mountain, 841 metres

which Brasilia, an entirely new city built in the interior to encourage the Brazilian people to move inland and develop areas with low population, became the capital.

Rio occupies an area of about 155 square kilometres (60 square miles) and stands on an alluvial plain between the mountains and the sea. In its early days health hazards were severe, and yellow fever and other tropical diseases were rife, but modern science and medicine eliminated these and Rio has become a rich and dynamic city.

A range of mountains called the

FACTS ABOUT
RIO DE JANEIRO

Founded 1565.
Population over 4·5 million.
Capital of the State of Guanabara.
Corcovado: 704 metres (2,310 feet) high.
Sugar Loaf: 395 metres (1,296 feet) high.

(2,759 feet) high, the skyline of which has earned it the name of the 'Sleeping Giant'. Between Gavea and the city lie internationally famous beaches, including the Copacabana, renowned for its tiled promenade and phalanx of modern hotels and places of entertainment which face the sea. Rio's superb harbour, and such events as the annual Carnival help to make the city a great tourist resort, but it is also the second most important industrial city in Brazil, after São Paolo. Its main industries are foodstuffs, luxury goods, printing and metallurgy.

ANTARCTICA
the frozen continent

Antarctica is the world's fifth largest continent and has an area of 13,209,000 square kilometres (5,100,000 square miles) on which the ice cap lies at a thickness averaging 2·4 kilometres (1·5 miles). Whether it was always like this is not known, but the discovery of the remains of flora and fauna found only in warmer climates suggests that either it was once warmer at the South Pole or perhaps Antarctica was part of one of the other continents, and later moved to its present position.

Although men like Weddell and Ross had sailed their ships as far as the ice would permit in the nineteenth century, little was known about Antarctica until the first expeditions across the ice-covered continent began at the end of the century.

The main objective was to reach the South Pole, but in the course of the competition which developed between the British explorers Scott and Shackleton and the Norwegian Amundsen, much was learned about the topography of Antarctica and

the climatic conditions.

Many hazards were encountered in the course of early exploration, and the heroic end of Scott and his companions on returning from the Pole after finding that Amundsen had reached it before them in 1911 is well known.

The earlier explorers were succeeded by others, like Vivien Fuchs, who crossed Antarctica with scientific discoveries in mind. Since then, the increase of scientific knowledge has become one of the main reasons for exploring

and living in Antarctica.

In order to advance this work, the twelve nations that have some claim to the Continent agreed in 1959 that all the studies carried on there would be of a non-military nature, and today this international cooperation and co-existence continues. In recent years Antarctica has become something more than a base for scientific studies; it has grown into a tourist destination visited by specially constructed ships which take visitors to gaze on the wonders of a unique continent.

Left
The snowmobile on the Beardmore glacier shows the modern way to travel in Antarctica.
Top
Mount Gaudry is one of the rocky peaks in the world's fifth largest continent that stretches across 13,209 million square kilometres (5,100 million square miles).
Above
Stray ridges of ice made Cap Evans almost inaccessible when Herbert Ponting, a member of Scott's expedition, took this photo.

FACTS ABOUT
ANTARCTICA

The fifth largest continent:
Area:
   13,209,000 square kilometres
   (5,100,000 square miles).
Average altitude:
   1,830 metres (6,000 feet).
Average thickness of ice:
   2,440 metres (8,000 feet).
Mean temperature:
   – 11°C. (– 12°F).

THE GREAT BARRIER REEF

largest coral formation in the world

Off the coast of Queensland in north-west Australia lies the Great Barrier Reef, 1,930 kilometres (1,199 miles) in length. The reef is not an uninterrupted ledge of coral, as it is broken up by islands and passages through which ships can pass: overall it acts as a barrier between the Pacific and the quiet lagoons which make the Reef a paradise for visitors.

There are six hundred islands on the Great Barrier Reef, as well as innumerable rocks and out-crops, the largest of which are visited by tourists and support a small resident population. About seventeen islands could be called resorts. Among them are Green Island, which has an underwater observatory set into the end of a jetty from the windows of which visitors may examine the teeming undersea life; Magnetic Island, which was so named by Captain Cook because of the deflection it caused to his compass readings; and Hayman Island, the largest

of them all. There are others whose names, such as Orpheus and Daydream, sum up their holiday images.

The huge area of the Barrier Reef provides scientists with ample opportunities to study marine life. There are research stations on Heron, One Tree and Lizard Islands, one of whose major research studies is the struggles of live coral against the depredations of the coral-eating Crown of Thorns starfish. Among the many other denizens of the sea under the watchful eyes of the marine scientists are the Green Turtle, of turtle soup fame, which is now a protected species, the Harlequin Tuskfish, the Raffles Butterfly fish and other colour-fully named inhabitants. The Reef also supports such deadly creatures as the stonefish, whose spines and attractive shell can be fatal to the unsuspecting ex-plorer, and the box jellyfish.

Above left
The Great Barrier Reef stretches over
207,200 square kilometres (80,000
square miles).
Above
Many of the islands on the Reef are
holiday resorts.
Right
Colonies of coral like these have been
building the Barrier Reef for
50 million years.

AYERS ROCK
the world's largest monolith

Near Alice Springs in the dead heart of Australia there rises a huge rounded rock reaching a height of 335 metres (1,099 feet) above the surrounding plain. Ayers Rock, discovered in 1873 by William Gosse, who named it after Sir Henry Ayers, Premier of Australia, has other remarkable qualities besides the fact that it is the largest rock in the world made of a single material. For most visitors, the strongest impression is of the Rock's colour, a reddish tone which covers the spectrum from yellow to purple according to the time of day and the weather.

In the caves below the Rock are aboriginal paintings. According to C. P. Mountford, who led the Arnhem Land expedition which studied the life and culture of aborigines, these are not of a religious nature. Nevertheless, to the aborigines of the area, the Rock is a symbol of life, and they believe that its situation on an otherwise flat earth was the result of great deeds by heroic ancestors.

The south side of the Rock is in the territory of the Pitjandjara people, in whose mythology is a legend of a battle between carpet snakes and their more venomous enemies, during which the land was stained by the blood shed in battle. The north side of the Rock is associated with another legend about the Hare Wallaby or Rat Kangaroo totem people. This tells of a hunting party who seized and killed a member of the Willy Wagtail totem tribe, but lost two of their men to giant dingoes who killed them while asleep.

The Rock can be climbed with the aid of the chains let into its surface and the summit provides a fine view of the plains below. More than 30,000 people visit this strange natural wonder every year.

FACTS ABOUT
AYERS ROCK

869·89 metres (2,854 feet) above sea-level.
38·62 kilometres (24 miles) south of Lake Amadeus.
2·6 kilometres (1⅗ miles) long by
1·6 kilometres (1 mile) wide.
Perimeter, 8 kilometres (5 miles).

SYDNEY OPERA HOUSE
unique architectural concept

Although the glittering white shell-shaped building that stands on Bennelong Point in Australia's beautiful Sydney Harbour is called the Opera House, it is in fact a culture complex which houses a theatre, concert hall, library, exhibition room and restaurants.

The idea of grouping together places concerned with entertainment is not new, but Sydney Opera House is the most original in concept so far constructed. Designer Joern Utzon's controversial plans for the Opera House were made public in 1957. When the building was finally and officially opened in the presence of Queen Elizabeth II in 1973, he had long since resigned from the project, his designs having been considerably modified in the meantime.

The site on Bennelong Point faces the famous Sydney Harbour Bridge and is surrounded on three sides by water. The complex stands on a podium built of 125,000 tons of concrete and 6,000 tons of reinforced steel. On this are three shell systems, one housing the Concert Hall which seats 2,700 people, another the Opera House with 1,550 seats, and the third the restaurants. Also on the podium are a Drama Theatre, and a Music Room.

The Concert Hall is made of granite, concrete and glass, and the wall behind the stage is faced with pink brushbox panelling. On the side facing the harbour, a foyer gives a superb view over the water, a view which is echoed in Australian artist John Olsen's mural, *Homage to Five Bells*. In the auditorium, the circular centre-point ceiling has twenty-one giant acrylic sound reflection panels suspended from the apex.

In contrast to the light decor of the Concert Hall, the Opera House is darker in colour and covered with a pleated plywood ceiling. Three strip panels suspended by cables help to give the Theatre superb acoustic qualities.

The total complex cost $A102 million, much of which came from a public lottery in which Australians could buy weekly tickets. For their money, the Australians have got one of the finest cultural centres in the world, and one of the most original pieces of architecture.

Far left
The Sydney Opera House is the focus of attention in Sydney Harbour. The podium on which it is built is 95 metres (312 feet) wide at the land end and 183 metres (600 feet) in length.
Inset
The halo's hanging over the auditorium in the concert hall improve the acoustics.
Above
The tallest of the highly original shells enclosing the Opera House and Concert Hall is 67 metres (221 feet) above sea-level.

FACTS ABOUT SYDNEY OPERA HOUSE

Site of Opera House:
   1·81 hectares (4½ acres).
Podium:
   95 metres (312 feet) wide at land end; 182·88 metres (600 feet) in length.
Highest shell:
   67·35 metres (221 feet) above sea-level.
Concert Hall:
   121·92 by 53·63 metres (400 by 176 feet), in area.
Opera House:
   107·28 by 39 metres (352 by 128 feet) in area.

NEW ZEALAND'S MOUNTAINS
South Pacific wonderland of snow and ice

Most people do not associate snow-covered mountains and glacial fiords with the South Pacific, and in this respect New Zealand's South Island is unique. The centre of it all is Mount Cook in the Southern Alps, in Canterbury, which at 3,764 metres (12,349 feet) is the highest point in the country. This sheer peak, though not among the giants of the world summits, is nevertheless a challenging one. The mountains of New Zealand are a popular training ground for mountaineers, and it is no coincidence that the conqueror of Everest, Sir Edmund Hillary, is a New Zealander.

In the Alps there are other high peaks, such as Mount Aspiring,

snow fields, deep lakes and glaciers, the largest of which is the Franz Joseph Glacier. Several major rivers rise in the Alps also.

Further south lies a wild land of sheer rocky mountains and fiords, best approached from the sea as the early navigators did. Captain James Cook sailed by here in 1770 and moored his ship at Pickersgill Harbour in 1773 to effect some repairs. Although an inhospitable region, New Zealand's fiord land attracted early settlers; the first house erected by a European was built in Milford Sound and, it is said, it was here that the sound of bagpipes first fell on the ears of the startled natives.

The Sound was named by a Welsh seal hunter called John Grono, no doubt in nostalgic memory of Milford Haven, and is dominated by the sheer pyramidal shape of the 1,695-metre (5,560-foot) Mitre Peak. The lower slopes of the mountains are heavily forested, because of the heavy rainfall, which averages 508 centimetres (200 inches) a year. Here there is much wildlife, including rare species of birds such as the Flightless Takahe with its blue and green plumage and red beak, and the Kakapo.

The land of fiords extends over some 3,023,713 acres and with the central mountainous region, forms an area of rare beauty among Pacific Islands.

Left
The wild landscape of the Cleddau River, Milford Sound area in the Fjordlands National Park.
Above
Mount Cook is the spectacular centrepiece of Southern New Zealand's national park. The Tasman glacier, 29 kilometres (18 miles) long, is another famous beauty spot.

NEW ZEALAND'S VOLCANIC PLATEAU

the Maori's sacred mountain

In the middle of Tongariro National Park in New Zealand's North Island rises Ngauruhoe, the sacred mountain of the Maoris and the most active volcano in New Zealand. According to Maori beliefs, volcanoes are warriors who were suitors of the beautiful Pihanga. The maiden favoured only one of them – Tongariro – so the others departed under cover of darkness to other parts of the island.

Tongariro rises to 1,960.3 metres (6,458 ft) and has a series of craters on its 8-by-3.2-kilometre (5-by-2-mile) summit. It last erupted in 1954–5. Tongariro is not entirely alone on New Zealand's 365.7-metre (1,200-foot) volcanic plateau, however. To the south is Ruapehu, a multiple

volcano 2,796·5 metres (9,175 feet) high with a crater lake. In 1953 the ash wall of the lake gave way and tons of water, carrying rocks and lava, poured down the Wanganui River carrying away a bridge and a crowded train in which 151 people died.

The fantastic volcanic region has its share of geysers, mud pools and hot springs. One of the largest of the geysers, Waimangu, the black geyser, is temporarily inactive, but used to shoot water 487 metres (1,600 feet) into the air.

In the midst of the desolation of volcanic rocks there are also forests and lakes, including Lakes Rotorua and Taupo, the largest. Near the former are the three most extensive geyser fields in the world, including Tikitere, known as Hell Gate because of the spectacular thermal activity there.

Rotorua is the home of the Arawa Maoris, who used the boiling pools for cooking and recognised the therapeutic properties of the volcanic mud. Although the Arawas were massacred by the Hongi chief, who provided his men with muskets, this strong and resilient people have grown to be the most populous among the urban Maori populations of New Zealand.

Another wonder of the North Island to the west of the volcanoes are the Waitomo Caves near Hamilton. In these caverns millions of glow worms illuminate the caves with their eerie light.

Far left
This geyser in the Rotorua thermal region provides visitors with an impressive spectacle when it erupts.
Below left
Sinter terraces, caused by silicate deposits, are another natural wonder of the volcanic plateau which rises 366–609 metres (1,200–2,000 feet) above sea-level on New Zealand's North Island.
Below
The hot springs at Ketetahi were used by the Maoris for their healing properties. These are near Tongariro's 1,968-metre (6,458-foot) volcano.

FACTS ABOUT NEW ZEALAND'S VOLCANIC REGIONS

North Island:
114·67 square kilometres (44·281 square miles) in area.
Central volcanic plateau:
365·76–609·6 metres (1,200–2,000 feet) high.
Ruapehu volcano:
2,796·5 metres (9,175 feet).
Egmont volcano:
2,487·6 metres (8,260 feet).
Ngauruhoe volcano:
2,290·5 metres (7,515 feet).
Tongariro volcano:
1,960·3 metres (6,458 feet).

Key to the Wonders of the World
in this book

•60

1. Stonehenge
2. The Tower of London
3. Durham Cathedral
4. Windsor Castle
5. St Paul's Cathedral
6. Mont St Michel
7. Île de la Cité
8. The Château de Chenonceaux
9. Versailles
10. The Eiffel Tower
11. The Centre Georges Pompidou
12. The Rhine Valley
13. Cologne Cathedral
14. Neuschwanstein Castle
15. The Roman Forum
16. Pompeii

17. Venice
18. Assisi
19. The Scrovegni Chapel
20. The Vatican City
21. The Acropolis
22. The Caves of Altamira
23. The Alhambra
24. El Escorial
25. The Kremlin
26. The Winter Palace
27. Istanbul
28. The Jungfrau Railway
29. Monaco
30. The Pyramids
31. Thebes
32. The Aswan High Dam
33. The Suez Canal
34. Mount Kilimanjaro

35. The Victoria Falls
36. The Okavango Swamp
37. Baalbek
38. Petra
39. Persepolis
40. Ispahan
41. Jerusalem
42. Mount Everest
43. The Caves of Ajanta
44. The Taj Mahal
45. Borobudur
46. Angkor Wat
47. Shwe Dagon
48. The Hôryû-ji
49. The Great Wall of China
50. Peking
51. The Fort at Lahore
52. Hong Kong

53. Chichen Itzá
54. The Grand Canyon
55. The Niagara Falls
56. Manhattan
57. Las Vegas
58. Disney World
59. Mount Palomar
60. Easter Island
61. The Galápagos Islands
62. Machu Picchu
63. The Iguazu Falls
64. Rio de Janeiro
65. Antarctica
66. The Great Barrier Reef
67. Ayers Rock
68. Sydney Opera House
69. New Zealand's Mountains
70. New Zealand's Volcanic Plateau

Horseshoe Point, the Grand Canyon,
United States of America.